Beriev's Jet Flying Boats

Yefim Gordon, Andrey Sal'nikov and Aleksandr Zablotskiy

Original translation by Sergey Komissarov

MIDLAND

An imprint of
Ian Allan Publishing

Beriev's Jet Flying Boats
© 2006 Yefim Gordon, Andrey Sal'nikov
and Aleksandr Zablotskiy
Edited by Dmitriy Komissarov

ISBN (10) 1 85780 236 5
ISBN (13) 978 1 85780 236 8

Published by Midland Publishing
4 Watling Drive, Hinckley, LE10 3EY, England
Tel: 01455 254 490   Fax: 01455 254 495
E-mail: midlandbooks@compuserve.com

Midland Publishing is an imprint of
Ian Allan Publishing Ltd

Worldwide distribution (except North America):
Midland Counties Publications
4 Watling Drive, Hinckley, LE10 3EY, England
Telephone: 01455 254 450   Fax: 01455 233 737
E-mail: midlandbooks@compuserve.com
www.midlandcountiessuperstore.com

North American trade distribution:
Specialty Press Publishers & Wholesalers Inc.
39966 Grand Avenue, North Branch, MN 55056, USA
Tel: 651 277 1400   Fax: 651 277 1203
Toll free telephone: 800 895 4585
www.specialtypress.com

Design concept and layout by
Polygon Press Ltd (Moscow, Russia)
Line drawings by the Beriyev TANTK

This book is illustrated with photographs
by Yefim Gordon, Dmitriy Komissarov,
Dmitriy Pichugin, the late Sergey Skrynnikov,
David Oliver, as well as from the archives
of the Beriev TANTK, Yefim Gordon,
Andrey Sal'nikov and Aleksandr Zablotskiy.

Printed in England by
Ian Allan Printing Ltd
Riverdene Business Park, Molesey Road,
Hersham, Surrey, KT12 4RG

Visit the Ian Allan Publishing website at:
www.ianallanpublishing.com

Contents

Introduction 3

1. OKB-49's Jet Firstling 5
2. The First Success 21
3. Proud Bird of the Sea 49
4. 'Little Brother' 75
5. On the Seven Seas:
   Ocean-Going Seaplane Projects 93

   Line Drawings 100
   Colour Photographs 112

Title page: The second prototype of the A-40 ASW amphibian ('20 Red') displays its elegant lines.
This page: An infrequently seen (and impressive) formation of three Beriev amphibians – left to right, Be-12P-200 '00046', Be-200 RA-21511 and A-40 '20 Red' – at the Hydro Aviation Show-2000 at Ghelendjik.

Front cover: The first prototype Be-200 makes a demonstration flight at the MAKS-2001 airshow.
Rear cover, top: Another view of the A-40 in a demonstration flight; **bottom:** Be-200ChS RF-32515, the first example to enter service with EMERCOM of Russia, on final approach.

Introduction

The Taganrog Aviation Scientific & Technical Complex named after G. M. Beriyev (the Beriyev TANTK – *Taganrogskiy aviatsionnyy naoochno-tekhnicheskiy kompleks*) was founded in 1934. Gheorgiy Mikhailovich Beriyev was appointed head of the Central Design Bureau of Seaplane Construction (TsKB MS – *Tsentrahl'noye konstrooktorskoye byuro morskovo samolyotostroyeniya*) which had been set up in the city of Taganrog on the Black Sea.

In the course of the seventy years of its existence the Beriyev TANTK has made a significant contribution to Soviet (later Russian) aircraft construction, first and foremost in the development of seaplanes. The MBR-2 short-range maritime reconnaissance aircraft, a single-engined flying boat of wooden construction, entered Soviet Navy service in 1933. It was followed by two shipboard (catapult-launched) seaplanes – the KOR-1 (alias Be-2) floatplane (which was built along conventional lines and also had a landplane version) and the KOR-2 (Be-4) flying boat. These were introduced into Navy service in the late 1930s and successfully flew combat sorties during the Great Patriotic War of 1941-45.

In the period spanning from the 1940s to the 1960s the Beriyev design bureau – then known as OKB-49 (*opytno-konstrooktorskoye byuro* – experimental design bureau) – developed several seaplanes intended for defending the nation's maritime borders. These were aircraft of worldwide renown: the Be-6 reconnaissance, patrol and bomber flying boat, the Be-10 turbojet-powered flying boat filling the same roles and the Be-12 twin-turboprop anti-submarine warfare (ASW) amphibian – the biggest in its class at that time. These aircraft remained in service for a long time, and had good performance and seaworthiness characteristics corroborated by dozens of world records. Development of these aircraft placed the Soviet Union at the forefront of world seaplane construction, laying the foundation of Russia's present-day position in this field.

In 1968 the design bureau produced the Be-30 (Be-32) commuter airliner; it was not put into production for political reasons, losing out to the Czechoslovak LET L-410 Turbolet. Twenty-five years later this programme was reactivated; in its new Be-32K version the

aircraft was shown at the 1995 Paris Air Show where it attracted much interest on the part of aviation specialists.

In that same year of 1968 G. M. Beriyev had to retire due to health reasons. He was succeeded by Aleksey Kirillovich Konstantinov as head of OKB-49.

In the 1970s and 1980s the scope of the design bureau's activities became much broader. Those years saw the development of strategic weapons systems; these were the A-50 airborne warning and control system (AWACS) aircraft and the Tu-142MR communications relay aircraft for extra-long-range communication between ground or airborne command posts and submerged missile submarines. Both were derived from existing baseline aircraft created by other OKBs (the Ilyushin IL-76MD transport and the Tupolev Tu-142M ASW aircraft respectively). The scientific and technical experience accumulated by the Beriyev TANTK enabled it to undertake development of a new generation of amphibian aircraft featuring a unique combination of high performance and seaworthiness characteristics. 1986 saw the first flight of the A-40 amphibian, the world's biggest jet-powered aircraft of this class. The perfection of its design was confirmed by 148 world records.

In 1990 Ghennadiy Sergeyevich Panatov was appointed Chief Designer and main administrator of the Beriyev TANTK; in 1992 he was promoted to General Designer and Chief of the Design Bureau. His advent in these posts marked a new epoch in the his-

The founder of the Beriyev company, General Designer Gheorgiy M. Beriyev, whose name is eponymous with Russian seaplane design.

tory of TANTK. Work was started on the development of multi-purpose amphibian aircraft intended for civil duties and having considerable export potential; they would later earn appreciation from customers and high appraisal on the part of specialists. In 2002 Valentin Vladimirovich Boyev was appointed General Director of the Beriyev TANTK. Contacts were re-established with the Russian Ministry of Defence and foreign customers.

A late-production MBR-2*bis* flying boat (characterised by the M-34 engine, recontoured hull and rounded vertical tail) flies a bombing mission during a pre-war naval exercise.

Above: A production Be-6PLO ASW aircraft of the Soviet Naval Air Arm coded '14 Yellow' on Taganrog Bay in 1958 (note the magnetic anomaly detector boom).

Above: The first prototype of the Be-8 experimental liaison amphibian. The retracted landing gear is clearly visible. This elegant aircraft did not enter production.

Since 2003 Viktor Anatolyevich Kobzev is the company's leader.

In addition to the fulfilment of defence contracts the Beriyev TANTK is working on civilian programmes. Development has been completed of the Be-200ChS multi-purpose civilian amphibian which is currently in series production at the Irkut Corporation. The Komsomol'sk-on-Amur Aircraft Production Association (KnAAPO) is manufacturing in series the Be-103 light amphibian capable of carrying five passengers; aircraft of this type have been delivered to the USA, and the Be-103 has recently won Chinese and Brazilian type certificates. Projects under development include the Be-112 and Be-101 amphibians.

The Beriyev TANTK is engaged in studying and projecting prospective giant amphibious aircraft with an all-up weight in excess of 1,000 tonnes (2,205,000 lb). Such aircraft will be able to deliver cargoes and passengers over big distances at altitudes and speeds typical of land-based aircraft, while making use of the transport infrastructure of the existing sea ports.

At present the Beriyev TANTK may well be regarded as the world's only aircraft constructor to specialise primarily in the design of seaplanes. Falling back on their unique experience gained in the course of several decades, the Taganrog designers are creating truly outstanding specimens of aviation hardware which hopefully will find employment in and outside Russia. This book deals with the jet-powered types developed by the company over the years.

A production Be-12 ASW amphibian of the Soviet Navy ('53 Yellow') takes off. The Be-12 shared the gull-wing layout of the Be-6, which earned it the popular name Chaika (Gull).

Chapter 1

OKB-49's Jet Firstling

R-1 Experimental Seaplane (*Izdeliye* R)

In the mid-1940s all the leading aviation powers of the world were actively introducing turbojet propulsion in land-based aviation. Understandably enough, priority was given to military aviation. The question of creating a turbojet-powered flying boat for combat duties also came on the agenda.

Albeit Gheorgiy M. Beriyev and his OKB-49 design bureau were occupied with design work on the piston-engined Be-6 flying boat, the General Designer was already pondering over the layout of his first jet. All the more so since Colonel-General Ye. N. Preobrazhenskiy, Commander of the Naval Aviation, was urging the development of new seaplanes; in this he was supported by Fleet Admiral Nikolay G. Kuznetsov, Commander-in-Chief of the Soviet Navy.

In May 1947 Beriyev, at his own initiative, started development of a turbojet-powered flying boat for maritime reconnaissance duties. It was a monoplane with a two-step planing bottom, featuring unswept gull wings,

a single fin-and-rudder and a high-set horizontal tail. Two Rolls-Royce Nene centrifugal-flow turbojets, each delivering 2,200 kgp (4,850 lbst), were mounted on the wings as high above the water as possible. Beriyev envisaged a speed of 750-800 km/h (466-497 mph) and a range of 2,000-2,500 km (1,243-1,554 miles) for his new machine. The defensive armament was to comprise a twin-cannon rear turret and a four-cannon installation in the nose. The bomb load in an overload configuration was estimated at 2,000 kg (4,410 lb). The jet-powered seaplane was to be equipped with the Gals (Tack) radar.

The Navy supported this initiative of OKB-49, albeit the tempo of work on the project was slowed by the fact that in 1947 Fleet Admiral Kuznetsov was removed from his post and then, in early 1948, suffered reprisals together with his closest associates.

Nevertheless, on 12th June 1948 the Soviet Council of Ministers issued directive No.2061-803ss calling for the development of

a turbojet-powered seaplane. The aircraft, which received the in-house designation '*izdeliye* R', was to be powered by two Soviet-built RD-45 engines (Soviet copies of the Nene); its design performance included a maximum speed of 750-800 km/h at an altitude of 5,000 m (16,400 ft), a technical range of 2,000 km (1,243 miles) and a service ceiling of 12,000 m (39,370 ft). *Izdeliye* (product, or article) such-and-such was/is a commonly used codename for Soviet/Russian military hardware items. The R apparently stood for *reaktivnyy* – jet-propelled. The seaplane was primarily intended to fill the maritime reconnaissance role, with a secondary role as a bomber able to carry bombs weighing up to 1,000 kg (2,205 lb) apiece in overload configuration. As regards the basic performance figures (for example, the maximum speed), the 'R' aircraft was on a par with the McDonnell FH1 Phantom and the Grumman F9F Panther, which were the main US carrier-borne fighters at the time, to say nothing of the

An artist's impression of the *izdeliye* R flying boat from the project documents, showing the gull wings, the extensively glazed blunt nose with no radar, the retracted outrigger floats and the lack of the fin/tailplane fairing.

Above: The nose of the *izdeliye* R's full-scale mock-up, showing the revised shape and reduced glazing (due to the installation of the Koors radar) and the port forward-firing cannon with the fairing removed.

piston-engined Grumman F8F Bearcat. On the other hand, the range was clearly insufficient for a maritime reconnaissance aircraft. However, the reader should bear in mind that at that time Iosif V. Stalin was preoccupied primarily with the 'strong defence of the USSR's maritime frontiers'; he often reiterated that '...we are not going to wage war near the US coastline'.

Under the terms of the Council of Ministers directive the aircraft was to be submitted for the state acceptance trials in December 1949. It should be noted, however, that at that time the staff of OKB-49 was quite small. There were no departments; the biggest team –

the one responsible for the hull design and led by V. A. Gherasimov and his deputy A. A. Klitsov – numbered fewer than 30 persons. The team responsible for the wing and tail unit design (led by B. A. Dybin, with V. K. Filippov as his deputy and P. D. Galitskiy as chief of the tail unit subdivision) consisted of 20 persons. The team dealing with the control system (led by V. N. Batalin) together with the group responsible for hydraulics and pneumatics (led by N. G. Revunov) numbered no more than 15 persons. In addition, there were teams for the powerplant (Morozov, Kochetkov), for electrics and radio equipment (Kudziyev, Grin'ko) and for the general equip-

ment (Belenovskiy). A. S. Korytin headed the section for preliminary design, his associates were A. K. Konstantinov and A. G. Bogatyryov. A. N. Kesennikh was responsible for structural strength, while V. P. Terent'yev was the chief of the structural strength team; Panich was the chief of the flight test facility. Some specific structural strength issues were the responsibility of I. P. Lebedev and A. M. Spichkin. In the meantime, the work on the Be-6 was going on in parallel; not surprisingly, this soon caused the work on the jet-powered 'R' aircraft to lag behind schedule.

By the stipulated time Beriyev OKB was in a position to submit only a full-scale mock-up of *izdeliye* R to the customer. In this connection one more Council of Ministers directive was issued; dated 10th June 1950 and bearing the number 2474-974ss, it shifted the deadline for submitting the aircraft for state acceptance trials by one year. The directive called for VK-1 turbojets (an uprated version of the RD-45) to be fitted and the tail turret to be equipped with 23-mm (.90 calibre) cannons instead of the 20-mm (.78 calibre) cannons originally envisaged.

A mock-up of the *izdeliye* R flying boat featuring a revised layout was presented to the mock-up review commission in the period between 21st and 24th March 1951. The appraisal was generally positive; the remarks made by the military included a demand that the range of compatible bomb types be expanded and the possibility of carrying two AMD-500 anti-shipping mines be considered. It was stated that the range of the aircraft fell short of the specifications issued by the Naval Aviation; the OKB's chief G. M. Beriyev contested this view, emphasising that the range met the technical requirement incorporated in the CofM directive. Debates on this issue between the Naval Aviation Command and the leaders of OKB-49 lasted until the very end of work on the *izdeliye* R.

In its final design configuration the flying boat, already bearing the official designation R-1, had a take-off weight of 17 tonnes (37,485 lb). It was powered by two VK-1 turbojets with a take-off thrust rating of 2,700 kgp (5,950 lbst) located at the joints between the wing centre section and the outer wing panels. To ease maintenance of the aircraft on the ground and afloat, the engines' air intake assemblies and side panels of the engine cowlings were hinged. The open cowling panels were stressed to serve as work platforms for engine maintenance. Provision was made for attaching jet-assisted take-off (JATO) bottles underneath the rear ends of the engine nacelles.

The first prototype of the R-1 seaplane was completed in November 1951 and submitted for manufacturer's flight tests at the OKB's water aerodrome at Taganrog. Colonel

Another view of the mock-up, showing the port inboard flap, the JATO booster bottle under the engine nacelle, the boarding ladder (for use when afloat) and the beaching gear.

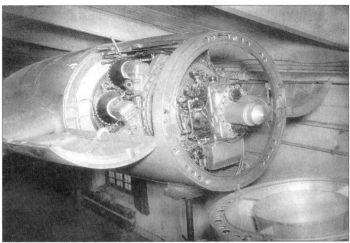

Left: Front view of the mock-up, showing the navigator's station glazing (note the optical bombsight), the cannons and the shape of the planing bottom.
Right and above right: The hinged air intake assemblies and cowling panels doubling as work platforms afforded good access to the engines.

Ivan M. Sookhomlin, a pilot from the Navy's NII-15 (Research Institute No.15), was appointed project test pilot. On 22nd, 24th and 25th November high-speed water runs were conducted; everything went smoothly, with no signs of anything untoward. Normally, the aircraft would be cleared for the first flight after water runs at speeds up to 70% of the take-off speed had been performed success-fully. Within this range of speeds the R-1 behaved normally, but when the crew attempted a run at 80% of the take-off speed (above 165 km/h, 103 mph), this was accom-panied by pitching oscillations so violent that the aircraft was literally kicked out of the water. On one occasion the machine pitched up almost into a vertical position and would have crashed, had it not been for the instan-taneous reaction of the pilot.

Detailed examination of the incident revealed that the designers were confronted for the first time with a completely new phe-nomenon that was later called the 'hydro-dynamic instability barrier'. In an attempt to find a solution to this problem the designers changed the balancing of the elevator and the stabiliser incidence. The water runs resumed as early as 27th November, but the measures effected proved to no avail; with the Sea of Azov becoming icebound (on 7th December) the tests were suspended until the spring of 1952.

During that period the specialists of OKB-49 and hydrodynamics experts from the Central Aero- & Hydrodynamics Institute named after Nikolay Ye. Zhukovskiy (TsAGI – *Tsen**trahl**'nyy aero- i **ghid**rodina**mich**eskiy insti**toot**) tried unsuccessfully to 'overcome the barrier', and the runs undertaken on 13th, 15th, 18th and 19th April gave the same unsatisfactory results as in the previous year. Further changes were introduced into the bal-ancing of the elevators and ailerons; still, a new series of high-speed runs on 18th and 19th May brought no improvement. The next stage involved measures intended to ensure venting of the planing bottom; this purpose was served by three pairs of openings in the planing bottom behind the main step and by the open camera window; in addition, a spring in the rudder spring tab was replaced by a push-pull rod. The aircraft thus modified resumed its runs on 21st May, but, again, with no positive results. After this, the camera win-dow was replaced by a fixed air scoop intended to create air pressure behind the main planing step.

The manufacturing drawings for the installation of the venting system air scoop were prepared as a matter of urgency during a weekend. During runs conducted on 24th May with the air scoop open the pitching oscillations of the aircraft became less pro-nounced, reverting to full strength with the air scoop closed. Thus, a measure of progress had been achieved. On 29th May, equipped

Left: A separate mock-up of the starboard outer wing, showing the retractable outrigger float carried on tandem struts.

Below left: The rear fuselage of the mock-up, showing the powered twin-cannon tail turret and associated observation/aiming blisters; the latter apparently incorporate bulletproof glass panes. Note the tail beaching gear unit with steering handle attached aft of the water rudder.

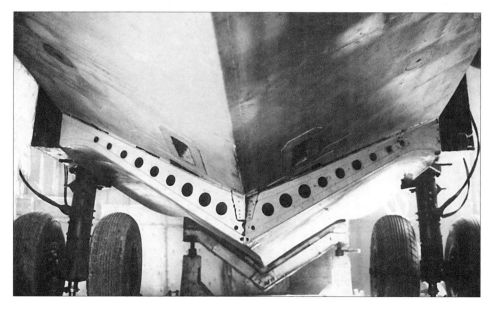

Bottom left: This view of the R-1 prototype jacked up (with the beaching gear in place) shows the venting orifices in the rear wall of the main planing step and two more orifices aft of it. These were introduced in an effort to cure the R-1's longitudinal instability at high speeds.

with the new air scoop located between fuselage frames 29 and 31, the R-1 conducted more or less stable planing runs at speeds up to 196 km/h (122 mph). It was decided to attempt a first flight on the following day.

On 30th May 1952 the R-1 became airborne, flown by test pilot I. M. Sookhomlin and flight engineer S. I. Kondratenko. In the air, tail buffeting set in at speeds in excess of 370 km/h (230 mph), and on touchdown the flying boat started porpoising, making three uncontrollable short bounces off the water surface. Nevertheless, the main goal had been achieved – the first Soviet turbojet-powered seaplane had taken to the air at last.

In the meantime, the designers of OKB-49 together with TsAGI specialists kept on devising means of counteracting the aircraft's buffeting in flight and longitudinal instability during take-off and landing. Intensive flight testing continued throughout the summer of 1952; in these flights, different revisions of the hull/rear fuselage contours were tested, as were various alterations to the wing high-lift devices. The engineers tried changing the stiffness of the spring in the rudder spring tab. Fairings were installed on and deleted from the gunner's lateral sighting blisters and the tail turret, T-shaped profiles and plates of different sizes were riveted to the trailing edge of the rudder, and the outrigger floats were provided with fairings. Still, the results of these modifications were unsatisfactory as ever.

Finally, after numerous experiments with models, it became clear that at high speeds prior to take-off a pocket of partial vacuum appeared behind the main planing step; the resulting pressure fluctuations caused pitching oscillations, ejecting the aircraft from the water at the wrong moment. It was decided to make the height of the step equal to 10-12% of the beam (instead of 2-3%, as was the case with piston-engined seaplanes which had appreciably smaller speeds of planing prior to take-off). With a high planing step, the jets of water arising during aquaplaning could not reach a level higher than the chines of the hull and thus prevent the ambient air from entering the space under the planing bottom

Left: Two 100-kg bombs under the starboard inner wing of the *izdeliye* R mock-up.

Above: The instrument panels in the pilot's cockpit of the *izdeliye* R mock-up.

behind the main step; this eliminated the possibility of the vacuum arising. In addition, the main (forward) step was moved aft 300 mm (11¹³⁄₁₆ in), the retractable venting system air scoop was replaced by a larger fixed one, and some of the venting openings were transferred to the vertical wall of the step; changes were also made to the bullet fairing at the fin/tailplane junction and to the rudder.

The R-1 underwent these modifications in October-November 1952 concurrently with the repairs of the damage it had suffered in a landing incident on 3rd October 1952. That occasion was the first solo flight in the R-1 by test pilot G. I. Boor'yanov who had recently graduated from a test pilot school; prior to that flight he had made two familiarisation flights on 26th September. During the landing, the aircraft started porpoising at 190 km/h (118 mph) and was thrown into the air to a height of 4 m (13 ft), with a heavy landing as a result (the G forces in the forward fuselage peaked at 10.6). As related by eyewitnesses (who were many, since the incident took place during a lunch break in full view of the plant's entire staff), the aircraft plunged into the water in a fountain of spray, only the vertical tail remaining visible. Ingesting a generous 'mouthful' of water, the engines quit, and the flying boat surfaced and rocked serenely on the water in complete silence broken only by the hiss of water evaporating from the hot engine nacelles. At a glance, it appeared that after all this the machine was a write-off; yet the R-1 proved to have such strength reserves

that it emerged from the incident with relatively minor damage.

After the repairs and all the modifications, between 30th November and 4th December the test pilots managed to perform several high-speed runs without scoring any notable success, before the ice caused the testing to be postponed until the spring of 1953. By that time everyone realised that all thinkable deadlines for submitting the aircraft for state

acceptance trials had been broken, and nobody could guarantee that the machine's faults would be cured in the following year of 1953.

All this touched off an 'enquiry' which took place at a meeting in Moscow chaired by Dmitriy F. Ustinov, who then held the post of Minister of Defence Industry. The meeting was attended by representatives of the Ministry of Aircraft Industry (MAP – *Ministerstvo*

Here the R-1 is seen undergoing ground tests. The centrifugal air blowers connected to the boxy structure attached to the planing step create a vacuum in order to check the efficiency of the venting system.

aviatsionnoy promyshlennosti), TsAGI, the Flight Research Institute named after Mikhail M. Gromov (LII – **Lyot**no-is**sle**dovatel'skiy insti**toot**) and other organisations and institutes. OKB-49 was represented by Chief Designer Gheorgiy M. Beriyev and the leading specialist in hydro- and aerodynamics A. K. Konstantinov. Minister of Aircraft Industry Mikhail V. Khrunichev suggested right away that the work on the *izdeliye* R seaplane be closed down; this could well be followed by a decision to disband the design bureau. However, the more pragmatically minded Ustinov decided to give Beriyev an opportunity to develop his machine, tasking him at the same time with the development of a more advanced jet-powered seaplane.

A certain part in the adoption of this decision was played by the attitude of Commander of the Naval Aviation Ye. N. Preobrazhenskiy who in June 1953 wrote in his letter to the Soviet Council of Ministers: '*...I find it expedient to use the prototype R-1 seaplane as an experimental aircraft for developing the aero- and hydrodynamics of a new aircraft; to refrain from building a second prototype and to entrust Comrade Beriyev with a new task of developing a flying boat powered by two jet engines...*' He was supported by Fleet Admiral Nikolay G. Kuznetsov, who by then had once more been appointed C-in-C of the Navy. In September 1953 Kuznetsov wrote to the then Minister of Defence Nikolay A. Boolganin: '*...Chief Designer Beriyev should be tasked with developing a new flying boat/amphibian powered by two turbojet engines and intended for reconnaissance missions and torpedo/bomb strikes against enemy warships and transport vessels'.*

The new seaplane was to have a maximum speed around 950-1,050 km/h (590-653 mph), a service ceiling of 16,000 m (52,490 ft), a service range up to 3,500 km (2,175 miles). It was to have seagoing properties enabling it to take off and land at a sea state with waves up to 1.5 m (5 ft) high. As early as 8th October 1953 the Council of Ministers issued directive No.2622-1105ss on the development of a new seaplane which received the designation '*izdeliye* M' – the future Be-10.

Flight tests of the R-1 jet-powered seaplane, now relegated to experimental status, resumed on 18th July 1953. In addition to other changes, the machine was fitted with

Top left: A view of the R-1's fuselage decking after the modifications made in May 1952. The retractable air scoop of the planing step venting system assisting take-off is closed.

Above left: Here the scoop is open.

Left: Close-up of the rather crude enlarged non-retractable air scoop fitted when the original design proved inadequate.

improved high-lift devices (extension flaps instead of slotted flaps). The venting of the planing bottom was thoroughly reworked; now air was supplied through two openings into a zone where the rarefaction was at its highest. The pressure in the venting ducts was measured by a specially developed gauge for measuring the pressure fluctuations. A full-scale mock-up of a new tail unit with swept-back tail surfaces was manufactured, but it was never built in hardware form. The seaplane proved to be quite stable during take-off and alighting, the aircraft left the water gently, without pitching down at the moment of lift-off. The unstick speed was 200 km/h (124 mph), the alighting speed was 185 km/h (115 mph)

Upon completion of the tests the R-1 prototype was used as a flying testbed and a training seaplane until February 1956, when test pilot M. Vlasenko performed a crash alighting in Ghelendjik Bay with the machine hitting a sand bank. After that the aircraft was not repaired; for a while (at least until 1959) it remained at the Ghelendjik test facility until finally scrapped.

The R-1 in Detail

Type: Twin-engined experimental flying boat. The airframe was of all-metal construction. The crew of three comprised a pilot, a navigator and a gunner/radio operator.

Fuselage: Two-step boat hull of basically oval cross-section with a V-section planing bottom; the first step had a V planform, the

Top: The R-1 (coded '5 Yellow') makes a high-speed run, showing off its distinctive 'dog nose' radome and the bullet fairing at the fin/tailplane joint.
Centre and above: Extension flaps were fitted at the final stage of the tests. Note that the sighting blisters have been removed and the tail turret faired over.

Above: The R-1 on the slipway at Taganrog on its beaching gear, showing the floats on the twin-wheel main units. The curvature of the hull chines is clearly visible.

The slight area-ruling of the engine nacelles is discernible in this view. The stripes on the hull in line with the cockpit and ahead of the observation blisters appear to be photo reference marks for judging the height of the spray.

two sections by the engine nacelles, the outer sections being larger) and one-piece ailerons featuring trim tabs and spring tabs. The ailerons were aerodynamically balanced and fitted with twin mass balances on ventral struts.

The wings featured outrigger floats carried on tandem struts; the floats retracted outward to form wingtips. The floats were hydraulically actuated, with electromechanical emergency extension.

Tail Unit: Cruciform cantilever tail surfaces. The *vertical tail* was slightly swept and featured a one-piece fin with a large root fillet and a one-piece rudder. The unswept *horizontal tail* of trapezoidal planform had zero dihedral and comprised fixed-incidence stabilisers, with a bullet fairing at the fin/tailplane joint, and one-piece elevators. The control surfaces were fitted with trim tabs, aerodynamic balances and mass balances; in addition, the rudder was provided with a spring tab.

Undercarriage: Beaching gear only, intended for ground handling, placing the aircraft afloat and beaching it. The beaching gear comprised the twin-wheel main units and a single tailwheel with a steering bar. The main units were fitted with twin detachable floats to ensure their flotation.

Powerplant: Two Klimov VK-1 non-afterburning turbojets with a take-off rating of 2,700 kgp (5,950 lbst) apiece. The VK-1 had a single-stage centrifugal compressor (with dual inlet ducts), nine straight-flow combustion chambers, a single-stage axial turbine and a subsonic fixed-area nozzle. The engine featured an accessory gearbox for driving fuel, oil and hydraulic pumps and electrical equipment. Starting was by means of an ST2 or ST2-48 electric starter.

The engines were installed ahead of the wing leading edge in area-ruled nacelles and fitted with long extension jetpipes. Each engine was mounted on a truss-type bearer via four attachment points: two trunnions on the sides of the compressor casing and two lugs in the upper part of the engine. Each nacelle comprised an annular forward section (air intake assembly), the hinged cowling panels and a large fairing integrated into the wing structure; the air intake incorporated a parabolic centrebody carried on cruciform struts.

For ease of maintenance, on the ground and afloat, the air intake assembly and side cowling sections could hinge downward, the cowling panels serving as work platforms for engine maintenance. Provision was made for attaching RATO bottles underneath the engine nacelles.

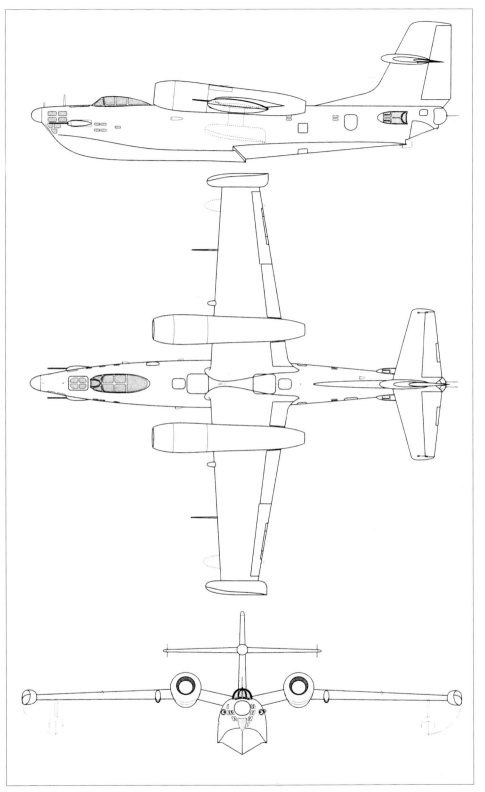

A three-view of the projected R-2. Note the cockpit located on the aircraft's centreline.

Control System: Conventional manual (unassisted) control system featuring push-pull rods, control cranks and cable linkages. Flight in automatic mode was ensured by an AP-5 autopilot whose servos were switched to the cable linkages of the control system.

Fuel System: All fuel was carried in two bladder tanks with a total capacity of 8,470 litres (1,863.4 Imp gal) housed in tandem in the fuselage under the wing centre section. The fuel was fed to each engine from its own service tank with the help of a PN-45T pump. An emergency fuel jettison system was provided.

One more view of the R-2 mock-up in 1952, showing the open access panels.

Hydraulics: The hydraulic system worked the flaps, outrigger floats and camera port doors. Hydraulic pressure was provided by engine-driven pumps; emergency extension of the flaps and the closing of camera hatches were effected hydraulically by means of a hand-driven pump.

Electrics: 27 V DC primary electric system. The circuitry used a single-wire layout, the airframe acting as the 'neutral wire'; the wiring was not shielded. DC power was supplied by two GSR-900 engine-driven DC generators, with two 12AS-65 storage batteries as a back-up. Equipment using AC received its energy supply from two MA-1000 converters. The system of circuit protection against overloading and short circuits was decentralised, with circuit breakers at the crew workstations.

De-icing System: Hot-air de-icing on the wing and tail unit leading edges and engine air intakes, using engine bleed air. The cockpit windshield was electrically de-iced.

Pressurisation / Air Conditioning System: The compartments housing the crew workstations were pressurised, with an air conditioning system maintaining the required microclimate in the cabins. The air for the air conditioning system was tapped from one of the engine compressors. In addition, the crew workstations were provided with an oxygen system.

Fire Suppression System: The powerplant was fitted with a fire warning system, a fire extinguishing system incorporating carbon dioxide bottles, and a system for pressurising the tanks with inert gas to prevent fire or explosion if pierced by bullets or cannon shells.

Avionics and Equipment:
Flight and navigation equipment: The aircraft was equipped for day and night operation in fair and adverse weather. Flight and navigation equipment comprised a Koors radar in the extreme nose, an NK-46B navigation indicator (*navigatsionnyy ko'ordinahtor*), a DIK-46 flux-gate compass, an OSP-48 instrument landing system (*oboroodovaniye slepoy posahdki* – blind landing equipment) comprising an ARK-5 Amur automatic direction finder (*avtomaticheskiy rahdiokompas*), an RV-2 Kristall low-altitude radio altimeter (*rahdiovysotomer*) and an MRP-48 Dyatel (Woodpecker) marker beacon receiver (*markernyy rahdiopriyomnik*), RV-10 high-altitude radio altimeter and other instruments.

Communications equipment: RSIU-3 Klyon (Maple) UHF command radio, RSB-5 communications radio with wire aerial stretched between the fin and a mast aft of the cockpit, AVRA-45 emergency radio and SPU-14 intercom (*samolyotnoye peregovornoye oostroystvo*).

IFF equipment: Magniy-M (Magnesium-M) interrogator and Bariy-M (Barium-M) transponder.

Photographic equipment: The aircraft featured a versatile installation for oblique photography fitted with an AFA-33/100 camera (*aerofotoapparaht*); it could be trained at depression angles between –5° and –30° (in 5° increments) through hatches on both sides of the fuselage. Vertical daytime photography could be done by means of AFA-33/100, AFA-33/75 and AFA-33/50 cameras; vertical night-time photography was possible by means of an NAFA-3S/50 camera (*nochnoy aerofotoapparaht*) through a camera hatch in the hull's bottom.

The photographic installation, as well as the opening and closing of the camera hatches, was controlled remotely from the navigator's cockpit.

Maritime equipment: The aircraft's maritime equipment was stored in the navigator's cockpit and included a bottom anchor with a 30-m (98-ft) cable, an anchor winch, a floating anchor, a hook with a 15-m (50-ft) rope, a grappling hook, towing slings and a bilge pump. For the purpose of anchoring the aircraft, mooring it to a buoy or a post, or towing, the boat was provided with a hatch in the upper decking of the forward hull, belaying cleats, and a stern hook.

Armament: The cannon armament comprised two fixed forward-firing 23-mm (.90 calibre) Nudelman/Richter NR-23 cannons with 100 rpg on the forward fuselage sides, and a tail barbette fitted with two 23-mm Shpital'nyy Sh-3 cannons with 200 rpg.

The pilot trained his weapons through the ASP-3N gunsight. The tail barbette was remote-controlled by the gunner/radio-operator from his workstation; the PP-2 sighting station was placed in the beam blisters.

Bomb armament was carried on underwing bomb racks. Its weight varied in different

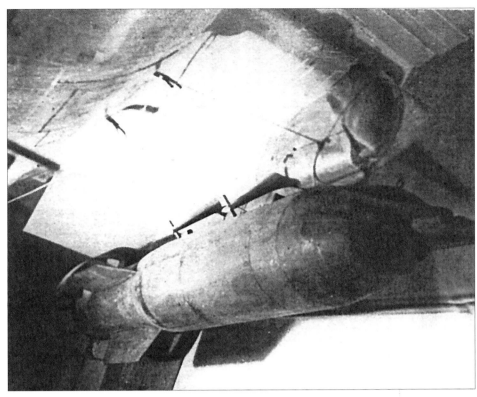

Above: A dummy RAT-52 rocket-propelled torpedo suspended from a beam-type rack under the R-2 mock-up's wing.

The cockpit of the R-2 mock-up in 1952.

Top and above: The side consoles in the cockpit of the R-2 mock-up.

Emergency and rescue equipment comprised one LAS-3 inflatable dinghy and three SAZh-43 life vests.

R-2 Seaplane (Project)

In parallel with the refinement of the R-1, design work went ahead on the second version of the *izdeliye* R flying boat – the R-2 seaplane, a full-scale mock-up of which was presented to Naval Aviation representatives on 30th July 1952. Actually, it was a mock-up of the forward fuselage, because the wings, the tail unit and the rest of the boat hull were identical to those of the R-1.

The main changes incorporated in the R-2 were as follows:

• new Klimov VK-5 engines were installed;

• the forward pressurised cockpit received a new layout;

• the antenna of the Koors radar was moved forward;

• the pilot's cockpit canopy was located on the aircraft's centreline;

• the navigator's station had greater glazing area;

• the forward-firing cannon installations were placed outside the pressurised cabin;

• the weapons range was expanded to include even the latest RAT-52 rocket-propelled torpedo, which was not yet cleared for Soviet Navy service.

The VK-5 was an uprated and improved derivative of the VK-1A. It had a nominal rating of 2,760 kgp (6,090 lbst), a take-off rating of 3,100 kgp (6,835 lbst), a specific fuel consumption of 1.015 kg/kgp·hr (lb/lbst·hr), so that, despite the reduction of the total fuel capacity from 8,470 litres (1,863 Imp gal) to 8,200 litres (1,804 Imp gal), the technical range was increased to 2,400 km (1,490 miles). This enabled the designers to affirm that they had taken into consideration the remarks made by the military, albeit that was obviously not the case. In turn, chief of the 9th Directorate of the Naval Aviation Major-General M. Kruglov ordered that the aircraft be given an effective (not technical) range of 2,400 km. (Technical range is a distance which the aircraft can cover from take-off to landing by using up as much of its fuel load as possible, while the effective range is a distance which the aircraft can cover allowing for the fuel spent during the start-up and trial run of the engines, taxying, take-off, landing manoeuvre, landing, taxying after landing, and the fuel reserves.) Since the military had already presented their new requirements by issuing a specification for the development of the 'M' combat seaplane, the R-2 project did not progress further than the drawing board.

Specifications of the R-1 Seaplane

Length	19.9 m (65 ft 3½ in)
Height	7.1 m (23 ft 3½ in)
Wing span	20 m (65 ft 7½ in)
Wing area, m² (sq ft)	58 (624)
Maximum all-up weight, kg (lb)	20,300 (44,760)
Maximum useful load, kg (lb)	1,000 (2,205)
Maximum speed, km/h (mph)	800 (497)
Service ceiling, m (ft)	11,500 (37,730)
Range with a maximum fuel load, km (miles)	2,000 (1,243)

options within a maximum of 1,000 kg (2,205 lb). The navigator aimed and dropped the bombs with the help of the OPB-5SN optical bombsight.

Crew Escape System: The pilot and the navigator were provided with ejection seats. To aid the evacuation of the aircraft, the top decking of the boat hull incorporated a jettisonable cover of the navigator's hatch and a jettisonable canopy of the pilot's cockpit. The gunner/radio operator evacuated the machine through an escape hatch in the rear hull.

Chapter 2

The First Success

Be-10 Flying Boat Prototype
(*Izdeliye* M)

By early 1953 it had become clear that the R-1, the first Soviet turbojet-powered flying boat, was already obsolete and putting it into series production was pointless. As for the revised R-2 version, it appeared that this machine would never leave the drawing board.

The main 'customer' for the products of the Taganrog-based design bureau was by no means satisfied with this state of affairs. In September 1953 Naval Aviation Commander Ye. N. Preobrazhenskiy submitted to Defence Minister Nikolay A. Boolganin a proposal that Chief Designer of OKB-49 Gheorgiy M. Beriyev be tasked with designing a new flying boat powered by two turbojets. His proposal was supported by Soviet Navy C-in-C Fleet Admiral N. G. Kuznetsov, who paid much attention to the development of naval aviation. As early as 8th October 1953 the Council of Ministers issued directive No.2622-1105ss calling for the development of a turbojet-powered flying boat which received the service designation Be-10 and the in-house designation 'izdeliye M'. It was intended for open-sea reconnaissance, bombing and torpedo attacks against ships from high altitudes,

minelaying, and bombing attacks against naval bases and coastal installations. The requirement stipulated that the machine should attain a maximum speed of 950-1,000 km/h (590-622 mph), have a range of 3,000 km (1,864 miles), a service ceiling of 14,000-15,000 m (45,920-49,200 ft) and be able to alight in a sea state with waves 1.5 m (5 ft) high and a wind speed of up to 20 m/sec (40 kts). The aircraft was to be submitted for state acceptance trials in November 1955. The second prototype was to be built in an amphibious version.

This work was of paramount importance for the Taganrog aircraft designers. Bearing in mind the failure of the R-1, the new flying boat simply had to be a success; if it failed, the design bureau could expect most serious repercussions. In projecting the Be-10, its designers made the most of the experience gained with the R-1/R-2. Particular attention was paid to a thorough study of the planing bottom contours. To begin with, experiments were carried out with small models in the TsAGI towing tank. This was followed by experiments with a large-scale model which was towed by a torpedo-boat in the mouth of

the Don River (near the village of Rogozhkino). Beriyev OKB employees Aleksandr K. Konstantinov, I. M. Zabalooyev and A. F. Shul'ga manned the torpedo boat in the capacity of experimenters; sometimes they were joined by G. M. Beriyev himself. In this way the OKB succeeded in developing fully the hydrodynamics of the future aircraft at high take-off speeds.

This was just one of the many problems facing the designers of OKB-49 during their work on the *izdeliye* M. The Be-10 had thrice the take-off weight and thrice the engine thrust of the R-1, being powered by two 7,260-kgp (16,000-lbst) Lyul'ka AL-7PB axial-flow turbojets. It had shoulder-mounted swept wings – for the first time in Soviet seaplane construction practice; the entire weapons load was carried internally and was dropped through a special hatch in the bottom of the hull. This was the first time that the OKB resorted to such a bold design feature.

For the purpose of fully integrating the aircraft's equipment with the airframe the Chief Designer set up a special group in the OKB's general arrangement team led by A. G. Bogatyryov; this *ad hoc* group was staffed with

An artist's impression of the *izdeliye* M (Be-10) from the project documents.

21

some twenty highly qualified designers coming from all subdivisions of the design bureau. The group resided in a separate room which the local wits immediately labelled 'Sochi-Matsesta' (after two well-known health resorts on the Black Sea coast). The point was that, due to the stringent security rules, the results of the group's activities were not on public view for some time, and a good many of the OKB's employees believed that their 'selected' colleagues were just having a good time, like summer resort guests.

At that time OKB-49 already had a set-up comprising specialised design teams dealing with different subjects. V. A. Gherasimov led the work on the design of the boat hull, B. A. Dybin was responsible for the wings and tail unit, A. I. Kochetkov and B. F. Titarenko for the powerplant. G. S. Sazonov was in charge of the armament, B. P. Salishchev was responsible for the electrical equipment, I. Ya. Belenovskiy for the general equipment, S. A. Atayants for the air conditioning system and the anti-icing system, V. F. Grin'ko for the radio equipment, V. N. Batalin for the flight control system and N. G. Revunov for the hydraulic and pneumatic systems. However, as the design work on the *izdeliye* M started, a new organisational structure of the OKB was adopted. The design teams became sections (departments) and were grouped into four design bureaux (KBs). KB-1 was headed by A. S. Korygin, KB-2 by A. N. Kessenikh, KB-3 by Kh. D. Kudziyev and KB-4 by A. K. Konstantinov; G. S. Trishkin became Beriyev's first deputy. At the same time the number of

specialists was increased, and construction of a new building was started (the Beriyev OKB still resides in that building).

In the meantime, the employees had to work in temporarily adapted premises where the work conditions were far from satisfactory. The department for the boat hull design was obliged to work in a conference hall with a bare cement floor and a cement ceiling through which the molten tar from the tarred roof seeped in the summer and dripped onto the drawing boards. The hall was situated above a foundry and, when the metal was poured into the moulds, noxious fumes pervaded the place, forcing the designers to leave the hall in haste and open all windows, regardless of the weather.

Nevertheless, work proceeded quickly, and on 15th May 1954 the Conclusion on the ADP of the Be-10 powered by two AL-7 engines was endorsed. Between 7th June and 15th July 1954 a State commission reviewed the full-scale mock-up of the jet-powered flying boat. The same month saw the start of static testing of the *izdeliye* M.

Construction of the first flying prototype also got under way. Since OKB-49 did not yet have its own prototype assembly shop at that time, the assembly of large units and the final assembly of the aircraft took place in the workshops of the neighbouring aircraft plant No.86, which was then producing the Be-6 flying boat (A. N. Sobolev was the plant's director and S. M. Golovin its chief engineer). The construction of the Be-10 prototype proved to be quite a challenge for the pro-

duction plant which was fully committed to the series manufacture of another machine; yet, the prototype of the new jet-powered seaplane was completed as early as October 1955.

Until the advent of the Be-10 all prototypes produced by the Beriyev OKB were tested locally, at Taganrog Bay, which entailed an interruption in the testing as soon as the bay became icebound. Therefore, as early as 1949 Gheorgiy M. Beriyev personally started searching for a new water test site where flight tests could be conducted all year round. Having inspected the Black Sea coast from the air (as a passenger in the Be-8 liaison amphibian), Beriyev opted for the town of Ghelendjik where an excellent bay and a fairly good concrete-paved seaplane slipway previously used by a military unit were available.

It was to that site that the Be-10 seaplane was transported in a special floating dock between 1st and 13th November 1955 for conducting the flight tests. In Ghelendjik the aircraft's subassemblies were mated in a special rig, whereupon the manufacturer's tests started on 20th December.

The very first engine run revealed a dangerous phenomenon. The powerful exhaust gas jets impinging on the airframe caused vibrations of such magnitude that cracks appeared in various elements of the rear fuselage structure, nuts became loosened of their own accord, and pipelines and wiring bundles broke from their attachment points. In consequence, the engines' extension jetpipes had to be splayed out a further 3° from

An artist's impression of a Be-10 taking on fuel from a submarine.

the aircraft's sides, and certain structural elements of the boat hull and the tail unit had to be reinforced. This made it possible to reduce vibration to acceptable limits.

Coded '10 Red', the first prototype Be-10 took to the air for the first time on 20th June 1956. The aircraft was flown by a crew comprising pilot Lieutenant-Colonel V. V. Kuriachiy, navigator V. S. Fadeyev and radio operator G. V. Galyatkin. The flight lasted 20 minutes and proceeded normally, except for the fact that the aircraft made two small bounces during the alighting; as a result, the cover of the gunner/radio operator's emergency exit located on the planing bottom fell off and sank.

On its second flight the Be-10 was piloted by test pilot G. I. Boor'yanov who remained crew captain during the manufacturer's test phase. A total of 76 flights were performed at this stage, in which the aircraft logged a total of 83 hours 33 minutes. On 20th October 1958 the manufacturer's testing was completed and the joint state acceptance trials started that same day; they lasted until 20th July 1959. At this stage the first prototype was joined by the first production machine ('15 Red', construction number 8600101). The prototype was used for determining the aircraft's performance and seaworthiness and for checking out the powerplant and equipment, while the first production machine was used for testing the armament, photographic equipment and autopilot. By the time the trials ended, the prototype had logged 138 hours 33 minutes in 109 flights, and the first pro-

Specifications of the Lyul'ka AL-7 Engine

	AL-7 (design performance)	AL-7PB (actual performance)
Take-off thrust, kgp (lbst)	7,700 (16,978)	7,350 (16,207)
Specific fuel consumption in cruise mode, kg/kgp·hr (lb/lbst·hr)	0.79	0.83
Engine weight, kg (lb)	1,150 (2,540)	1,700 (3,750)

Above: The first production Be-10, '15 Red' (c/n 8600101), on its beaching gear. Note the striped photo calibration markings ahead of the engine air intake. Note the large spray deflectors on the nose.

This head-on view of the same Be-10 afloat shows to advantage the strong wing anhedral.

Comparative Performance of the Soviet Naval Aviation Aircraft

	Be-10	Tupolev Tu-16	Ilyushin IL-28
Powerplant	2 x AL-7PB	2 x AM-3	2 x VK-1
All-up weight, kg (lb)	48,500 (106,9403)	71,500 (157,660)	21,200 (46,750)
Weapons load, kg (lb)	3,360 (7,410)	9,000 (19,845)	3,000 (6,615)
Maximum speed, km/h (mph)	910 (566)	992 (616)	900 (559)
Service ceiling, m (ft)	12,500 (27,563)	12,800 (42,000)	11,950 (39,208)
Technical range with a normal bomb load, km (miles)	2,940 (1,877)	5,290 (3,288)	2,260 (1,404)
Crew	3	6	3

duction machine had logged 91 hours 31 minutes in 65 flights. The tests had to be suspended three times; on one occasion this was due to the aircraft moving from Taganrog to Ghelendjik, while the other two cases were caused by engine failures.

Note: The Be-10's seven-digit construction number system was fairly straightforward. For example, c/n 8600302 means year of manufacture 1958, MAP plant No.86 (as was often the case, the first digit was omitted to confuse hypothetical spies), production batch 003, 02nd aircraft in the batch. In the case of the Be-10 each batch contained up to five aircraft. The c/n was stencilled on the forward fuselage sides aft of the navigator's station glazing.

In the state acceptance trials protocol the Be-10 was recommended, with certain reservations, for introduction into Naval Aviation service in the reconnaissance and torpedo bomber role. However, it was noted that the performance fell short of the Naval Aviation's specifications. The aircraft had a maximum speed of 910 km/h (566 mph) instead of the required 950-1,000 km/h (590-622 mph), a service ceiling of 12,500 m (27,563 ft) instead of 14,000-15,000 m 45,920-49,200 ft) and an effective range of 2,895 km (1,799 miles) instead of 3,000 km (1,864 miles).

The main reason for the inadequate performance was the discrepancy between the engine's actual performance and the design figures (see table on the previous page). The test personnel also drew special attention to the frequent failures of the powerplant and the short time between overhauls (a mere 40 hours).

In the opinion of test pilots N. Sizov, M. Vlasenko and G. Boor'yanov, the seaplane had fairly good performance and seaworthiness characteristics which enabled it to operate at wave heights up to 0.8 m (2 ft 7 in); it could be flown by average-skilled pilots and could be recommended for operation by service units. The thrust/weight ratio was quite sufficient for continuing the flight with one engine shut down at an altitude of up to 6,000 m (19,680 ft) and an all-up weight of 43,000 kg (94,815 lb. The drawbacks, in addition to those noted above, included the following: take-off was impossible in crosswinds in

excess of 7 m/sec (14 kts), the AP-5-2M autopilot was not reliable enough and the view from the cockpit was inadequate. Furthermore, at speeds below 400 km/h (249 mph) the Be-10 had a tendency to flick into a right spin. The Koors-M radar installed on the aircraft had not passed its state acceptance trials by that time.

When assessing the tactical characteristics of the new jet flying boat, the Navy noted that the Be-10 had comparable performance to contemporary Soviet land-based jet aircraft (see table at top of page), and its tactical radius of action enabled it to fly missions against the carrier task forces of the potential adversary. However, the conditions and means of maritime warfare had changed substantially since November 1953 when the specific operational requirement (SOR) for the seaplane had been issued; guided missiles were becoming ever more important. Therefore the military were of the opinion that the combat use of the Be-10 armed only with torpedoes and free-fall bombs would be limited. Its combat envelope could be expanded only if the Be-10 was equipped to carry missiles.

Despite the numerous remarks and deficiencies noted in the state acceptance trials protocol, nobody ventured to contest the decision on putting the new turbojet-powered seaplane into production – a decision that had been taken before the completion of the trials, as was often the case. It was assumed that the machine could be brought to the required standard in the process of series manufacture.

Be-10 Production Flying Boat (*Izdeliye* M)

The Be-10 was series-built at the Taganrog Machinery Plant named after the Bulgarian

Communist Gheorgi Dimitrov (TMZD – *Taganrogskiy mashinostroitel'nyy zavod imeni Dimitrova*), or plant No.86, between 1958 and 1961. The production run, in addition to the prototype, totalled 27 machines. The production rate peaked in 1959 when 12 jet seaplanes were manufactured, tested and delivered to the Naval Aviation (by comparison, three machines were delivered in 1958, nine in 1960 and three in 1961).

The creators of the Be-10 paid great attention to the technological efficiency of their product. In the process of mastering production of the new seaplane unique items of equipment were introduced at plant No.86. These included hydraulic presses for manufacturing skin panels from sheet metal by stretching, electropneumatic devices for thermal treatment, and automatic and semi-automatic welding apparatus. In the airframe component build-up areas, jigs were erected in conformity with the subdivision of the boat hull into four sections. New production processes were mastered, such as simultaneous treatment of a batch of parts, the bending of pipes filled with a liquid, chemical milling and ultrasonic soldering. To make the hull watertight, for the first time in Soviet practice its assembly involved the use of the U-30MS brushable sealing compound instead of the Thiokol tape used previously. The airframe incorporated large panels made of duralumin alloy, which made it possible to reduce their weight and achieve greater manufacturing precision. AL-8 aluminium alloy optimised for injection moulding (*alyuminiy liteynyy*) was used for highly stressed structural elements (later this turned out to be the machine's undoing); cast parts made of 35KhGSA grade steel were also used.

Numerous problems arose in the course of preparations for the Be-10's series manufacture, and subsequently in the course of the actual production. However, they were solved promptly by the joint efforts of specialists from plant No.86 and the Beriyev OKB. A valuable contribution to this was made by production chiefs of both enterprises (A. I. Shamrov and N. K. Gavrilyuk respectively) and by the chiefs of the assembly workshops – A. Ya. Yegorov and N. D. Pribytkov, and later also I. Ya. Akopov.

The following maximum flight speeds for production Be-10s, depending on the altitude, can be found in technical documents:

Maximum Speeds Attained by Production Be-10s

Altitude, m (ft)	0 (0)	2,000 (6,560)	4,000 (13,120)	6,000 (19,680)	8,000 (26,240)	12,000 (39,360)
Max speed, km/h (mph)	650 (404)	760 (472)	840 (522)	885 (550)	870 (541)	840 (522)

Above: The Be-10 prototype was fitted experimentally with raised air intakes and extended inlet ducts meant to minimise spray ingestion. On this provisional installation the skin panels around the new inlet duct sections were not fitted and the curvature of the ducts is clearly visible.

Another view of the modified prototype moored to a buoy in Ghelendjik Bay. This view shows clearly the tail gunner's station and the DK-7 tail turret with the associated PRS-1 Argon gun ranging radar. Note the photo calibration markings on the nose and tail.

The bomb load or the load of mines and torpedoes in overload configuration was 3,300 kg (7,276 lb).

The testing and acceptance of production flying boats involved a good deal of flight incidents. On 29th June 1960 a Be-10 (c/n 9600403) came to grief at the plant's water airfield. The aircraft was performing a routine pre-delivery test flight, piloted by a Soviet Navy acceptance crew captained by test pilot Lieutenant-Colonel Yu. A. Tsirulyov. Dead calm reigned on that day. With no wind, the surface of Taganrog Bay turned into a veritable mirror; it proved extremely difficult to determine visually the distance to it at the landing speed of 210 km/h (131 mph). In this situation it would have been sufficient for a cutter carrying a mobile air traffic control station to make a 'run' on the alighting area of the airfield; the cutter's wake would have become a good visual aid to the pilot. Yet, nobody had thought of doing this, and Tsyrulyov misjudged his landing approach, flaring out prematurely and letting the aircraft sink to the surface from a greater height than required. As a result, the machine hit the water hard, suffering serious damage. Fortunately, the crew survived, but the gunner/radio operator Sergeant Major N. A. Avdeyenko was seriously injured, having prematurely freed himself from his harness.

On 25th May 1961 a Be-10 (c/n 0600701) crashed while performing a check-up flight in Taganrog; the aircraft was piloted by a crew captained by factory test pilot I. D. Zanin, Hero of the Soviet Union. The crash occurred on take-off, when the aircraft pitched up abruptly before reaching the unstick speed. The machine lifted off but then became uncontrollable and crashed. Hitting the water, the Be-10 broke its back in the main step area, the rear fuselage coming off. Still under momentum, the forward hull with the wings and engines continued its movement along the water, travelling several dozen metres, while the severed rear part of the hull assumed a nearly vertical position with the tail upwards. The fuel escaping from the ruptured tanks ignited. Radio operator/tester A. F. Lyashkov was the only survivor. Miraculously he managed to extricate himself from his cramped workstation in the tail and climb onto the fin, inflicting injuries to his leg muscles in the process. He was rescued by a cutter carrying the floating ATC station. Pilot I. D. Zanin and navigator B. A. Golovchenko remained at their workstations and were killed in the crash. During the investigation a surmise was voiced that during the take-off run a system pushing the pilot's seat aft prior to ejection went into action of its own accord, causing the pilot to haul back on the control column involuntarily and cause a premature lift-off. Eventually, however, the accident investigation board assumed that pilot error was the cause.

One more incident happened to an aircraft piloted by a crew captained by Colonel A. G. Yakovenko, a test pilot of the military acceptance team at plant No.86. Here is a description of the incident in his own words:

'This happened at an altitude of 6,000 m [19,685 ft] and at a speed of 900 km/h [559 mph]. I heard a sound like a gunshot. My first thought was 'engine trouble' However, when the sound was followed by resilient jets of air that broke their way into the cockpit and started lashing at my face, I realised that something had happened to the cockpit glazing. I informed the ground control about the situation and began a descent. I kept reiterating in my mind the passage from the flight manual warning that at speeds close to 400 km/h [248 mph] the aircraft was prone to flicking into a right spin. There was no reaction from ground control. The powerful air stream pushed the laryngophones from my throat to my neck and tucked them under the collar. I was deprived of communication both with the ground and with my crew. In these circumstances I could not even order the crew to eject. The roar of the jet engines, which was bad enough but kind of tolerable in the closed cockpit, now penetrated through the earphones of my flying helmet and attacked my eardrums in a sort of frenzy. Several times an idea struck my mind: I must give the order to eject, but how should I do this? However, when the navigator sitting in the lower section of the cabin began tugging at my foot, I took my hand off the control wheel for a few seconds and gave him a thumbs-up, showing him that everything was okay so far. The navigator understood my sign and informed the gunner/radio operator through the intercom that the captain was all right and was heading for a landing.

As the saying goes, it never rains but it pours. In the cockpit there was a blind flying hood intended to cover the windshield when pilots were trained in instrument flying. The air stream bursting into the cockpit pressed the blind against the windshield, and it resisted any effort to fold it away. Possibly at that moment, or maybe, later, a thought came to me: oh, with what relish would I tear away this rag and throw it in the face of the person who had thought of attaching it here! It blocked my forward view oh so much!

During the approach I noticed a white cutter going on its course on the sea. I decided

Three production Be-10s of the 318th Independent ASW Air Regiment at rest on Lake Pleshcheyevo where they were temporarily deployed for the 1961 Aviation Day flypast at Moscow-Tushino. Note the red trim on the wing and tail unit leading edges and the engine air intakes.

Above: Be-10 '10 Yellow' (c/n 8600302), seen here moored to a buoy at Ghelendjik during tests, featured extended engine nacelles with raised air intakes; the conversion was performed by plant No.86.

to alight along a line parallel to its course – should there be any trouble during the alighting, people from the boat would come to our rescue. When I heard the rattle of small waves against the bottom of the aircraft's hull, I understood that the alighting was successful. Imagine my surprise – the cutter which I had noticed from the air turned out to be no cutter at all but a big white motor vessel. The people on board waved their hands and white handkerchiefs at us merrily.

When the roar of the engines subsided I heard a message from the ATC chief over the radio ordering me to shut down the engines and wait for the arrival of a tugboat. Possibly, prompted by euphoria after the safe termination of the flight, or by the excitement caused by what had happened, I did not comply; instead, turning the seaplane in the right direction, I began taxying towards the water aerodrome. Not far from the slipway I shut down the engines. The people on the tugboat that approached us gazed at us in amazement but nobody asked any questions. My eyes were watering, but still I did observe a crowd of people on the shore. Apparently, the news about the incident must have spread very quickly all over the plant. An ambulance was parked near the slipway, and stretchers were placed on the ground near it. Pointing to them, I asked the flight controller:

– What's the purpose of all this?
The controller merely shrugged.

A three-quarters rear view of a Be-10 moored to a buoy. The tail turret appears to be dismantled. Again, only the aft tips of the outrigger floats are immersed.

– Tell the medical personnel they'd better give me a few ampoules of penicillin.

A physician on duty reached for her bag and, producing several ampoules, gave them to me. I put them in my pocket and went to change my clothing'.

Investigation into the causes of this incident revealed an extremely serious defect – cracks in the glazing of the cockpit canopy which could lead to explosive decompression at high altitude ending in a crash. As an emer-

gency measure, an attempt was made to solve the problem by dividing the one-piece transparency into two halves by a longitudinal frame member on top. This brought no positive result – the cracks continued to appear. It proved necessary to undertake a huge amount of research together with the All-Union Institute for Aviation Materials (VIAM – *Vsesoyooznyy instituut aviatsionnykh materiahlov*) concerning the use of oriented Plexiglas and the development of methods of

Above: Another aspect of the modified Be-10 c/n 8600302 at Ghelendjik. Note the circular window in line with the cockpit canopy replacing the two smaller windows usually found in the area.

The strong dihedral of the horizontal tail is evident in this view.

rier of this missile, had virtually stopped by then; at the same time the 'sea-going' Be-10 had a certain advantage over land-based strike aircraft, namely the ability to operate in areas lacking prepared airfields. Given the nuclear weapon delivery vehicle development concept characteristic for the mid-1950s, this capability appeared particularly valuable.

Since the K-12 missile was now the responsibility of a new organisation, on 12th September 1958 the Soviet Air Force issued to OKB-49 a new specification for the airborne missile system which received the designation K-12B (the B apparently was a reference to Beriyev). The system was intended for delivering strikes against major warships and transport vessels as well as naval bases.

In accordance with the requirements, the normal take-off weight of the carrier aircraft with one missile was to reach 48,500 kg (106,940 lb). The system's radius of action was to be 1,400-1,500 km (870-932 miles), the launch range being 90-100 km (56-62 miles) from an altitude of 10,000 m (32,810 ft).

Two years later, mock-ups of the flying boat's missile-carrying version designated Be-10N (*nositel'* – carrier) and of the missile itself were submitted to the Navy's mock-up review commission. The missile was designated K-12BS (the S probably stood for *samolyotnyy* – in this case, air-launched, because the initial version of the missile had been developed by a design bureau specialising in naval applications).

The new missile, large as it was and outfitted with complex electronic equipment, necessitated some changes in the design of the missile platform as compared to the baseline flying boat. The forward fuselage of the Be-10N up to frame No.18 was reworked to provide space for the installation of a new radar intended to control the missiles. To reduce weight and increase reliability, the weapons bay with its dorsal and ventral hatches was deleted, as was the whole bomb and torpedo armament and nearly all cameras. The nose-mounted cannons, the RV-17 radio altimeter and the Koors-L radar were also deleted. Instead, a new K-12U Shpil' (Spire, or Capstan) radar was installed in a large thimble radome supplanting the short glazing of the navigator's station; the new navigation equipment included the Veter-2 (Wind-2) Doppler speed and drift meter. To ensure the functioning of the new equipment consuming much energy, the capacity of the electric system was increased by installing an AC generator. The ASO-Be-10 passive self-protection system (chaff and flare dispensers) was replaced by the Avtomat-2 device. An RSIU-5 radio was fitted instead of the older RSIU-4. Provision was also made for installing the *Dyural'-LK* (Duralumin-LK) IFF system.

Above: Be-10s in Tushino parade colours anchored at Lake Pleshcheyevo. The nearest aircraft ('39 Yellow') may be c/n 0600504.

Above: The crews were delivered to and from the moored seaplanes by Soviet Navy speedboats. This shot gives a good detail view of the port engine nacelle.

The outrigger floats were also painted red (or at least had red tops). Note the fatter gun ranging radar radome of late-production aircraft.

The crew that flew the modified Be-10 (M-10) on its record-breaking flights in September 1961. Left to right: navigator V. M. Bogach, pilot G. I. Boor'yanov, radio operator V. P. Perebaylov.

The main armament of the new strike system consisted of one or two K-12BS cruise missiles suspended on pylons under the inner wings. Bearing in mind the peculiarities of piloting and the difficulties of taking off from water with a single missile attached, the missile was suspended under the port wing. The missile(s) could be hooked up both on the ground (with the aircraft resting on its beaching gear) and when the aircraft was afloat (from a special loader boat).

Defensive armament comprised the usual DK-7B tail turret with two AM-23 cannons which afforded traversing angles of ±65° and elevation angles of 60° up and 40° down. The turret was remote-controlled with the help of the PS-53K optical sighting station or the PRS-2 Argon-2 gun ranging radar.

The Be-10N armed with one K-12BS missile had a design maximum speed of 875 km/h (544 mph) and a service ceiling of 11,600-11,800 m (38,060-38,715 ft). The missiles could be launched at speeds between 700 km/h (435 mph) and the maximum speed, at altitudes in excess of 5,000 m (16,400 ft). The K-12U radar could detect a surface ship the size of a destroyer at a distance of some 150 km (93 miles). Depending on the flight profile, the launch was to take place at a distance of 40 to 93-110 km (25 to 58-68 miles) to the target. In other words, this very important performance parameter fell somewhat short of the stipulated maximum launch range of 100-120 km (62-75 miles). The design mean speed of the missile was 1,890 km/h (1,175 mph), the maximum value being 2,500 km/h (1,554 mph). The probability of hitting the target was estimated at 75-95%; direct hits by two K-12BS missiles were required to turn a destroyer into a 'destroyee'.

The weight of the missile, too, was rather far from meeting the specifications – it was as high as 1,900 kg (4,190 lb) instead of the stipulated 1,200-1,500 kg (2,650-3,310 lb). This played a considerable role in reducing the system's radius of action which, in the case of a single Be-10, was 1,250 km (777 miles) instead of the required 1,500 km (932 miles).

The ADP of the K-12B airborne strike system was submitted to GKAT's Scientific & Technical Council on 10th June 1959; it was approved on the whole, yet the project failed to reach the hardware stage. Some rather more promising airborne strike systems developed by other design bureaus suffered the same fate due to Khrushchov's particular predilection for land-based missiles.

Be-10S ASW Seaplane (Project)

The Beriyev OKB considered the possibility of developing an anti-submarine warfare version of the Be-10 that would be armed with the SK-1 Skal'p (Scalp) nuclear depth charge. This version, which failed to materialise, was designated Be-10S (the S was a reference to the Skal'p weapon).

Be-10U Target Designator Seaplane (Project)

The Be-10 served as a basis for a maritime over-the-horizon (OTH) target designator aircraft fitted with the Uspekh (pronounced *oospekh*, success) radar system; it was intended for detecting surface targets and passing the information to ship-based and shore-based missile installations. The aircraft itself bore the designation Be-10U (U denoting the word Uspekh). As in the previous case, this work did not reach the hardware stage and was discontinued by August 1960. Instead, the Uspekh system found use on the Kamov Ka-25Ts (*tseleookazahtel'*) shipboard OTH targeting helicopter.

Trainer Version of Be-10 (Project)

A dual-control trainer version of the Be-10 was developed, to be used for conversion training of pilots. The instructor's cockpit was located in the extreme nose, supplanting the navigator's station. Four shipsets of parts were manufactured in Taganrog and sent to Donuzlav, a naval base where the Be-10s were based,

Records Established on the Be-10 (M-10) Turbojet Seaplane

Record	Value	Pilot	Date
Speed over a 15 to 25-km (9.3 to 15.5-mile) track	912 km/h (567 mph)	N. I. Andriyevskiy	07.08.61
Speed over a 1,000-km (622-mile) circuit without cargo	875.86 km/h (544.35 mph)	G. I. Boor'yanov	03.09.61
Speed over a 1,000-km circuit with a cargo of 1,000 kg (2,205 lb)	875.86 km/h (544.35 mph)	G. I. Boor'yanov	03.09.61
Speed over a 1,000-km circuit with a cargo of 2,000 kg (4,410 lb)	875.86 km/h (544.35 mph)	G. I. Boor'yanov	03.09.61.
Speed over a 1,000-km circuit with a cargo of 5,000 kg (11,025 lb)	875.86 km/h (544.35 mph)	G. I. Boor'yanov	03.09.61
Altitude with a cargo of 1,000 kg (2,205 lb)	14,062 m (46,137 ft)	G. I. Boor'yanov	08.09.61
Altitude with a cargo of 2,000 kg (4,410 lb)	14,062 m (46,137 ft)	G. I. Boor'yanov	08.09.61
Altitude with a cargo of 5,000 kg (11,025 lb)	14,062 m (46,137 ft)	G. I. Boor'yanov	08.09.61
Altitude	14,062 m (46,137 ft)	G. I. Boor'yanov	09.09.61
Altitude with a cargo of 10,000 kg (22,050 lb)	12,733 m (41,777 ft)	G. I. Boor'yanov	11.09.61
Altitude with a cargo of 15,000 kg (33,075 lb)	11,997 m (39,362 ft)	G. I. Boor'yanov	12.09.61
Maximum payload to an altitude of 2,000 m (6,560 ft)	15,206.4 kg (33,530.1 lb)	G. I. Boor'yanov	12.09.61

Above: Navigator V. M. Bogach catches the hawser as the record-breaking Be-10 '40 Yellow' (c/n 0600505), alias M-10, is prepared for towing to the take-off position. The section of the nose immediately below the navigator's station glazing is a radome.

for the purpose of converting production aircraft into trainers *in situ*. However, research has not yet revealed any information as to whether any conversions actually took place.

Record-Breaking Version of the Be-10 (M-10)

A single production Be-10 coded '40 Yellow' (c/n 0600505) was converted into a record-breaking seaplane. The tail turret was replaced by a fairing, an additional pitot tube was installed on the fin, and spray fences were added for an attempt on a speed record. In documents sent to FAI the machine was presented under the designation M-10.

Twelve world records were established on the Be-10 in 1961. The record flights were performed at Donuzlav on 7th August 1961 by a crew captained by N. I. Andriyevskiy, Commander of the 318th OMPLAP (*Otdel'nyy morskoy protivolodochnyy aviatsionnyy polk* – Independent Maritime ASW Air Regiment). The crew also included navigator A. V. Bez-verkhniy and radio operator T. A. Fedorenko. On 3rd, 8th, 9th, 11th and 12th September of the same year record flights were performed by a crew captained by test pilot G. I. Boor'yanov (the crew also included navigator V. M. Bogach and radio operator V. P. Perebailov).

A retouched photo of the same aircraft under tow. Note the absence of the nose-mounted cannons.

In addition to the actual and projected versions of the Be-10 listed above, the OKB began development of a system for refuelling the aircraft at sea from a submarine, but this work was also discontinued when construction of the special Project 648 tanker submarine was terminated.

When the flying career of the Be-10 was approaching its end, one of the discarded machines was used for investigating the influence of salt water on the flying boat's airframe. The machine was kept afloat for a long time anchored to a buoy in Ghelendjik Bay. This work made it possible to work out

Above: The record-breaking aircraft on its beaching gear.

This view of the M-10 (Be-10 c/n 0600505) shows the fairing supplanting the tail turret and the extra pitot on the fin.

Above: The modified Be-10 starts up its engines before one of the record-breaking flights (note the puff of smoke from the turbostarter).

Above: The M-10 (Be-10 c/n 0600505) skims along the waves, approaching unstick speed.

The record-breaking Be-10 passes over the city of Taganrog.

recommendations concerning airframe protection against salt water corrosion, which were put to good use when designing the Be-12 amphibian. Interestingly, when the last Be-10s were already dead and gone, a postage stamp was issued with a Be-12 sporting a spurious Aeroflot livery – which this aircraft had never worn. To this day this prompts conjectures about the existence of a civil version of this flying boat which, in actual fact, never existed.

Over the Black Sea Expanses
In the summer of 1959 the second squadron of the 977th OMDRAP (*Otdel'nyy morskoy dahl'niy razvedyvatel'nyy aviatsionnyy polk –*

Opposite page, top and centre: Two more views of the same aircraft as it approaches unstick speed, trailing an impressive wake of spray.

Bottom: The M-10 is caught by the camera as it becomes airborne.

Independent Naval Long-Range Reconnaissance Air Regiment) of the Black Sea Fleet's Air Arm started converting from the Be-6 to the Be-10. The unit was based at Lake Donuzlav on the Crimea Peninsula. This regiment became the only service unit to operate the Be-10, and all production machines of the type were assigned to its two squadrons.

Mastering the Be-10 in the regiment involved a fair share of complications because the aircraft demanded greater piloting skills than its predecessor, the Be-6. The Be-10 did not forgive the error of prematurely increasing the angle of attack during take-off, and its alighting speed was more than 50% higher compared to that of its predecessor; therefore, highly skilled pilots were needed to operate it. Furthermore, the conversion was complicated by the absence of dual controls and a workstation for the instructor on the new flying boat. Therefore the pilots started with mastering a landing approach in a Be-6 with the flaps retracted to give a higher

approach speed; this was followed by familiarisation with taxying procedures, water runs at different speeds and familiarisation flights. In these flights the trainee pilot sat behind the instructor and watched his actions which were accompanied by the latter's comments over the intercom.

In different variants of the weapon complement the aircraft could carry three RAT-52 air-dropped rocket-propelled torpedoes, three IGDM induction hydrodynamic mines or APM air-dropped floating mines, 12 FAB-250 bombs or a single FAB-3000 bomb. In visual meteorological conditions the weapons were aimed with the help of the OPB-11KM bombsight coupled with the AP-5-2M autopilot. In adverse weather the Koors-M radar was used as a bombsight. It was also used for determining the aircraft's location during flights over the sea.

In 1961 the 977th OMDRAP was renamed, becoming the 318th Independent ASW Air Regiment (OMPLAP). In the summer of the same year the machine was demonstrated to

Above: A still from an old movie showing operational Be-10s anchored at Lake Donuzlav.

Above and below: The forward fuselage of Be-10 '41 Yellow' (c/n 0600601), showing the port nose cannon's blast deflector. In the lower view the navigator pops out of his hatch to supervise the towing.

the general public. Four Be-10s, piloted by Lieutenant-Colonel Andriyevskiy, Major Borisenko, Major Gordeyev and Captain Ponomarenko, made a formation flypast over the Neva River during the Navy Day festivities in Leningrad. At approximately the same time the Be-10 was demonstrated at the traditional Aviation Day air display at Moscow-Tushino. On that occasion the announcer of the Soviet Central Television referred to the jet sea-planes making a flypast as 'a detachment of flying cruisers'. These shows did not go unnoticed in the West; the flying boat received the NATO reporting name *Mallow* (in the 'miscellaneous' category).

During the Tushino air display the fresh-water lake of Pleshcheyevo near the town of Pereyaslavl'-Zalesskiy (not far from Moscow) became a temporary base for the flying boats. The aircraft were refuelled from usual tanker trucks driven onto the lake shore; refuelling hoses were laid to the aircraft with the help of lightweight wooden bridges. On the way back to Donuzlav one of the flying boats carried a rather unusual cargo – an upright piano was delivered to Taganrog, making use of an opportunity (at that time pianos, like many other things in the Soviet Union, were expensive and in short supply). However, contact with the fresh water of the lake brought an unpleasant surprise – the anti-corrosion coating of the hull bottom started flaking.

Gradually, as the flying personnel accumulated experience and improvements were made to the aircraft by OKB-49 and plant No.86, the machine became more predictable and easier to handle. Yet, the Be-10 continued to pose serious difficulties during take-off and alighting; even experienced pilots had trouble keeping the aircraft under control in these piloting modes. Therefore, unfortunately the flying boat's service career was marred by a series of fatal and non-fatal accidents.

Above: Be-10 '41 Yellow' (the same aircraft as on the previous page) makes a flypast at one of the air events in 1961.

Another scene from a show appearance. The Be-10 had a very distinctive silhouette when airborne, with those rakishly sweptback wings and tip floats.

Left: Be-10 '42 Yellow' (c/n 0600604?) under tow.
Note how the towing hawser is attached to the aircraft.

The first of these occurred on 14th October 1961 when pilot error caused the crash of a Be-10 piloted by Major Gordeyev, a participant in the Tushino display. Another Be-10 crashed fatally on 22nd May 1962; this was a machine piloted by Lieutenant (Senior Grade) Belov.

One more machine, coded '50 Yellow', crashed on 16th August 1961. On that day deputy squadron commander Captain Elyan made a flight in this aircraft and found nothing untoward with the aircraft's behaviour. After that a crew captained by Lieutenant (SG) Kooz'menko set off on a mission on the same flying boat. What happened next was similar to the episode with Zanin's crew in Taganrog in May 1961. During take-off Kooz'menko's machine stalled and crashed after an abrupt pitch-up, killing the pilot and the navigator. When the aircraft's wreckage was salvaged from the water, it transpired that the elevator trim tab had been set at 4° for pitch-up, although the flight manual required it to be set at only 2° (building on experience, the regiment's airmen had come to the conclusion that on this particular Be-10 the trim tab should be set exactly at 4°). This led the 'tin kickers' to conclude that the wrong trim tab setting was the cause of the crash. However, in a similar way to the investigation of the Taganrog crash, there were reasons to believe that the pilot's seat had spontaneously slid into the extreme rear position, causing an involuntary control input.

After this accident, Be-10 operations were suspended. Furthermore, cracks began to appear *en masse* in parts manufactured of the aforementioned AL-8 aluminium alloy. The use of this high-strength injection moulding alloy had helped improve the efficiency of production methods during the manufacture of aircraft. The AL-8 was widely used in stressed structural elements of the Be-10's airframe because VIAM had recommended its use in parts intended to meet particularly stringent demands as regards strength and resistance to salt water corrosion. However, in due course it became clear that the alloy had a propensity to develop, after some ten years of service, intercrystalline corrosion and corrosion-induced cracking when subjected to cyclic 24-hour fluctuations of ambient temperature during the operation of the aircraft; all of this had been overlooked. As a result,

Left and above left: A quartet of Be-10s passes over Soviet Navy warships anchored on the Neva River in Leningrad during the Navy Day festivities in August 1961.

Above and below: Two more views of the same 'diamond four' formation. The pilots maintained generous intervals between the aircraft.

corrosion started eating away at the flying boat's airframe.

In addition, by the end of the 1950s the use of free-fall bombs and torpedoes was definitely *passé*. The service introduction of ship-borne anti-aircraft missiles nullified the Be-10's chances to break through the AA defences and reach a position for a torpedo attack. New weapons and new tactics were needed. They emerged in the shape of anti-shipping cruise missiles, and the Naval Aviation command lost all interest in the Be-10. All these reasons combined were instrumental in prompting a decision to discontinue development of the seaplane and phase it out in 1963. The Be-10 was never officially adopted for Soviet navy service; these machines remained parked on the bank of Lake Donuzlav for quite a while until, in 1968, they were finally struck off charge and scrapped.

Unfortunately, not a single example of the Be-10 has survived. For a long time two such aircraft lay dumped in a remote corner of the factory airfield in Taganrog, and at one time an idea cropped up to place one of them on a plinth. Alas, both machines fell prey to the plan for scrap metal delivery. You never know what you've got 'til it's gone.

The Be-10 in Detail

Type: Twin-engined flying boat. The main mission of the aircraft was open sea reconnaissance, torpedo bombing from high altitudes and bomb attacks against ships. Additional tasks included minelaying, and bomb attacks in level flight against naval bases and coastal installations. The flying boat was intended for performing its combat missions in daytime and at night, in adverse weather conditions, in the open sea, both by single aircraft and by groups of aircraft.

The airframe was of all-metal construction. The crew of three comprised a pilot, a navigator and a gunner/radio operator.

Fuselage: Two-step boat hull of basically oval cross-section with a V-section planing bottom; the first step had a V planform, the second step was wedge-shaped, tapering to a point near the stern. The fuselage was divided into nine compartments by watertight bulkheads; the aircraft retained buoyancy with any two compartments flooded. The bulkheads incorporated doors which were hermetically sealed when closed. Spray guards

Top left, centre left and above left: Three views of the Be-10 from the 1961 Tushino flypast. Note the pale colour of the hull bottom coated with anti-corrosion paint.

Left: This view shows well the deep main step, the position of the water rudder and the fat radome of the PRS-2 Krypton gun ranging radar.

Above: Be-10s share the apron with a Be-6 at the seaplane base (flight test facility) of plant No.86 in Taganrog.

were fitted to the forward fuselage sides to prevent water ingestion by the engines.

The foremost and rearmost compartments were pressurised. The forward compartment housed the navigator's station (whose glazed dome formed the forward extremity of the fuselage) and the pilot's cockpit; they were accessed through the forward door to starboard and an entry compartment. The pilot's cockpit was enclosed by a bubble canopy featuring a fixed windshield (with curved triangular sidelights and a semi-ellipti-

cal optically flat windscreen), a jettisonable centre portion and a solid rear fairing. A dielectric radome for the Koors-M radar was faired into the nose contour below the navigator's station glazing.

The centre fuselage was flanked by the engine bays. It incorporated a weapons bay aft of the main step with watertight clamshell doors in the planing bottom; weapons loading took place through a hatch in the upper decking of the hull. The doors and locks of the bottom hatch were hydraulically actuated.

The aft compartment accommodated the gunner/radio operator's station with a powered cannon barbette and a gun ranging radar. It was accessed through a port side rear door and a central hatch. In addition, there were three camera hatches – two on the fuselage sides below the engine air intakes and one in the aft fuselage bottom.

All entry hatches on the outside of the hull and all internal passage doors, the cockpit canopy, the hatches of the navigator's and gunner/radio operator's stations, the

The centre fuselage, starboard engine nacelle and starboard wing root of a Be-10 coded '10 Yellow'. The main beaching gear units equipped with floats are clearly visible, as are the wing fences. Note the restraining clamps on the aileron.

weapons loading hatch and the ventral weapons bay doors, as well as the camera hatches, were sealed along the contour of the opening by inflatable rubber hoses. The air was fed into the rubber tubes at a pressure of 3 kg/cm² (42.8 psi) after the closing of the locks.

Wings: Cantilever shoulder-mounted gull-type wings built in three sections, with zero dihedral on the centre section and anhedral outer wings. Leading-edge sweep 35°. The wings had a two-spar torsion-box structure and were fitted with one-piece area-increasing slotted flaps. The one-piece ailerons located outboard of these were provided with electrically actuated trim tabs. The wingtips terminated in short pylons carrying non-retractable outrigger floats. Each outer wing had two prominent boundary layer fences designed to delay tip stall.

Tail Unit: Conventional sweptback tail surfaces of two-spar stressed-skin construction. The vertical tail had 35° leading edge sweep, consisting of a one-piece fin with a root fillet and a one-piece rudder. The horizontal tail featuring 40° leading-edge sweep and strong dihedral comprised fixed-incidence stabilisers and one-piece elevators. The rudder and the elevators were aerodynamically balanced and fitted with electrically actuated trim tabs. Control of the elevator trim tab was backed up by a cable linkage.

Undercarriage: For ground handling, putting the aircraft afloat and beaching it the aircraft was provided with a detachable beaching gear with non-braking wheels.

Powerplant: Two Lyul'ka AL-7PB axial-flow non-afterburning turbojets rated at 7,260 kgp (16,000 lbst). The AL-7PB was a single-spool turbojet featuring an intake assembly with a fixed spinner and 12 radial struts, a nine-stage compressor with a supersonic first stage, an annular combustion chamber with 18 vortex-type flame tubes, a two-stage turbine and a fixed-area nozzle. The compressor had bleed valves at the fifth and seventh stages.

Engine accessories were driven via a ventral accessory gearbox whose power take-off shaft was located aft of the compressor. Starting was by means of a TS-19A turbostarter – a small gas turbine engine driving the spool directly via a clutch (the term 'jet fuel starter' is not applicable, since the starter ran on aviation gasoline); there were two ignition units with centrifugal fuel spray nozzles and spark plugs in two of the combustion chamber's

Top, a Lyul'ka AL-7PB turbojet; above, a test rig featuring an AL-7PB complete with the Be-10's engine nacelle.

flame tubes. The engine had an all-mode hydromechanical fuel control unit (FCU) and a closed-type lubrication system with a fuel/oil heat exchanger.

Engine pressure ratio (EPR) 9.1; mass flow at take-off rating 114 kg/sec (251 lb/sec), normal turbine temperature at take-off rating 1,133° K, maximum turbine temperature 1,200° K. Specific fuel consumption (SFC) 0.97 kg/kgp·hr (lb/lbst·hr) at take-off power and 0.872 kg/kgp·hr in cruise mode. Length overall 3, 130 mm (10 ft 10⁵⁄₁₆ in), casing diameter 620 mm (2 ft 0³⁹⁄₆₄ in). Dry weight 1,746 kg (3,850 lb).

The engines were housed in conformal nacelles flanking the hull beneath the wing centre section, breathing through circular fixed-area air intakes and exhausting through outward-angled extension jetpipes. Large fairings were provided between the jetpipes and the fuselage. The front portions of the nacelles featured hinged cowling panels which doubled as work platforms, affording access to the engines for inspection with the aircraft afloat.

Control System: Conventional manual flight control system; rigid control linkages everywhere, with the exception of a small stretch of cable linkages within the control wheel column. The control system was not power-assisted; reduction of control forces in the yaw and roll channels was achieved by using spring tabs and trim tabs.

An AP-5-2M autopilot was fitted, with servos connected to the control linkages in a parallel layout. The water rudder was controlled by a power-assisted system slaved to the rudder.

Fuel System: The fuel load was 18,750 kg (41,335 lb), of which 11,000 kg (24,250 lb) were housed in two tanks in the hull and a further 7,750 kg (17,085 lb) in 16 wing tanks. All fuel tanks were bladder tanks; those in the hull had a protective self-sealing liner. Single-point fuelling was used. There was a provision for emergency jettisoning of the fuel from the wing tanks.

The aircraft was fitted with a system for filling the space in the tanks above the fuel level with a neutral gas; there was also a fire-extinguishing system.

Hydraulics: The hydraulic system worked the flaps, weapons bay doors/locks, camera port doors and cannon barbette. Hydraulic pressure was provided by engine-driven pumps.

Above right: The partially dismantled port engine nacelle of a Be-10 undergoing maintenance.

Right: This view shows how the Be-10's engine cowlings opened downwards to act as work platforms.

Here, the cowling is mostly removed and the engine is prepared for removal (lowering by means of a hand-driven hoist). Note the hefty engine bearer bracket and the ventrally located engine accessories.

Electrics: 27 V DC primary electric system. The power was supplied by two engine-driven DC generators. Back-up DC power was provided by a 12SAM-55 (28 V, 55 A·h) silver-zinc battery. In addition, there were single-phase and three-phase AC systems which served as sources of power supply for some systems and units.

Pneumatic System: The aircraft's pneumatic system had a working pressure of 150 kg/cm² (2,134 psi). Compressed air was supplied by two AK-150 compressors mounted on the engines, supplemented by compressed air bottles.

De-icing System: Hot-air de-icing for the wing and tail unit leading edges, engine air intake lips and the glazing of the crew cockpits.

Life Support Equipment: Normal crew operation at high altitudes was ensured by the pressurisation/air conditioning system which maintained the required microclimate in the pressure cabins. The system used bleed air tapped from the engine compressors. A centralised oxygen system was installed, with individual control panels at the crew's workstations.

Avionics and Equipment

Flight and navigation equipment: The aircraft was equipped for day and night operation in fair and adverse weather. Flight and navigation equipment comprised a Koors-M radar for detecting surface targets, an SP-50 *Materik* (Continent) ILS, an ARK-5 ADF, an RV-2 low-altitude radio altimeter, a Litiy-17M (Lithium) high-altitude radio altimeter and other instruments.

Communications equipment: RSIU-3M UHF command radio, RSB-70M long-range communications radio, AVRA-45 emergency radio and SPU-5 intercom.

IFF equipment: Kremniy-2 (Silicone) IFF transponder.

Electronic countermeasures equipment: ASO-2 chaff/flare dispensers.

Photographic equipment: For daylight vertical photography an AFA-33M/75, AFA-33M/50, AFA-33M/20 or AFA-NT-1 aerial camera was used; for night photography an NAFA-3S/50 was fitted. Oblique photography was performed with an AFA-33M/100 aerial camera. The photographic installation was remote-controlled from the navigator's station.

Maritime equipment: The maritime equipment included a bottom anchor with an anchor winch and an extra cable; two floating anchors; a grapnel with a casting rope; an anchor tab with a lock; a loud-hailer; plasters for repairing leaks in the hull; bilge pumps.

Armament: The weapons bay could accommodate offensive weapons. In different combinations the aircraft could carry torpedoes (three RAT-52 rocket-propelled torpedoes, as well as BRAT-500 or BRAT-1500 torpedoes), anti-shipping mines (three IGDM induction hydrodynamic mines, APM air-dropped floating mines, AMD-500M or AMD-2M mines) or bombs (12 FAB-250 bombs or one FAB-3000 bomb). Visual aiming was done with the help of an OPB-1KM bomb sight linked with the AP-5-2M autopilot. In adverse weather conditions, the Kurs-M radar was used for bomb aiming; it was also used for solving navigation tasks during flights over sea areas.

The dropping of weapons was effected electrically. An OPB-11S bombsight was used for bomb aiming.

Defensive armament comprised an aft-mounted remote-controlled barbette with two 23-mm (.90 calibre) Afanas'yev/Makarov AM-23 cannons; these were aimed by means of a PKS-53 gunsight coupled with a PRS-1 Argon radar. Two more AM-23s were mounted in a fixed forward-firing installation in the nose and fired by the pilot, using a PKI collimator gunsight.

Crew Escape System: Emergency escape equipment comprised K-22 ejection seats, SAZh-43P life vests, MPLK-49 parachutes with MLAS-1 individual life dinghies, and an LAS-5M five-man inflatable dinghy. For abandoning the aircraft in an emergency, the navigator had an escape hatch overhead and the pilot could use a hinged section of the cockpit canopy. The gunner/radio operator used a ventral escape hatch.

Specifications of the Be-10

Length	31.5 m (103 ft 4 in)
Height	10.2 m (33 ft 5½ in)
Wing span	28.6 m (98 ft 10 in)
Wing area, m² (sq ft)	130 (1,399)
Maximum all-up weight, kg (lb)	48,500 (106,940)
Maximum fuel load, kg (lb)	18,750 (41,340)
Maximum useful load, kg (lb)	3,360 (7,410)
Maximum speed, km/h (mph)	910 (566)
Unstick speed, km/h (mph)	300 (186)
Alighting speed, km/h (mph)	210 (131)
Service ceiling, m (ft)	12,500 (27,560)
Range with a maximum fuel load, km (miles)	2,895 (1,799)
Range with a maximum fuel load (reconnaissance), km (miles)	3,150 (1,958)
Endurance, hours	4.3
Endurance (reconnaissance), hours	4,6
Take-off distance, m (ft)	5,000 (16,400)
Alighting distance, m (ft)	3,100 (10,170)
Crew	3

which brought the various domestic civilian and military aircraft manufacturers under one roof—except that this was one of his so-called "national champions," controlled and bankrolled by the state.

The results continued to prove disastrous. By last year Russian aircraft production had plummeted to a grand total of seven, acknowledged by President Dmitry Medvedev as a "very sad figure." And the collective fleet continued to age—in the hinterlands, three-decade-old airplanes aren't uncommon—resulting in more and more tragedies, culminating with Smolensk.

It's been impossible for Medvedev to ignore this dynamic. As the hockey team was being burned alive, the president himself was, ironically, at Lokomotiv's home arena a dozen miles away, preparing to address Russia's political elite at an international policy forum. He had already proposed yet more reforms—these, for a change, made sense—after the Polish president's death, cutting the number of government-backed airlines and rescinding the foolish tariff, which allowed the remainder to rejuvenate their fleets with foreign-made aircraft. "The value of human life should be higher than any other logic, including supporting domestic manufacturing," Medvedev said at a press conference in Yaroslavl. (You can't keep a good apparatchik down: The tariffs remained in place for small planes, as well as certain midsize aircraft.) Since Smolensk the Kremlin has dished out still more directives, such as cutting the tiny regional airlines that fly very old planes.

Too often, though, the Kremlin is simply playing a game of Whac-A-Mole: In June, after a Tupolev-134 crashed, Medvedev ordered it grounded. In July it was an Antonov-24, so that model was grounded, too. Neither of which prevented September's crash of the Yak-42D.

In part that's because a two-decade

NOT READY FOR TAKEOFF

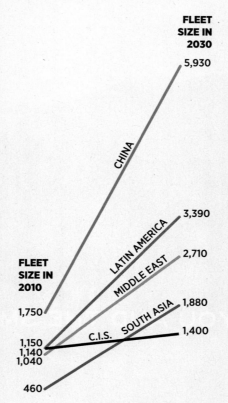

FLEET SIZE IN 2030

5,930 CHINA

3,390 LATIN AMERICA

2,710 MIDDLE EAST

1,880 SOUTH ASIA

1,400 C.I.S.

FLEET SIZE IN 2010

1,750

1,150
1,140
1,040

460

The Russian commercial aircraft market presents a $60 billion opportunity over the next 20 years, if foreign manufacturers can break in. The underserved demand is huge: Only 5% of the population in Russia and the former Soviet republics currently flies at all. Despite the potential, projections for growth in traffic and aircraft sales in the region lags other BRIC nations. Asia-Pacific air traffic, for example, is forecast to grow 7% a year through 2030, Russia and the former Soviet states 4.2%. According to Boeing, two-thirds of the 1,080 jets expected to be sold across the former Soviet Union over the next 20 years will be single-aisle and regional jets to serve an expected increase in budget carriers. Only 40 jumbo jets may be delivered. Aeroflot has 22 of Boeing's 787 Dreamliners slated for delivery through 2017. Compare that with 180 jumbo jets expected to be sold in the Middle East. None of the airframe giants will find a wide-open market. Bombardier notes in its most recent forecast that the Russia aircraft market is "not liberalized, and access to the marketplace is tightly controlled, particularly for new aircraft."

problem, rooted in bad policy, has sunk it roots widely. These old planes came from a half-dozen firms, which produced a half-dozen models each, which means that pilots often are flying unfamiliar machines: The copilot of the Sept. 7 crash had been untrained in flying that model. Given the lousy safety culture among mechanics and pilots—more than one has been discovered to be inebriated in the cockpit—this is a terrifying prospect.

Furthermore, it's an industry that needs volume to improve. That "sad" seven-aircraft figure means that Russian planes, says one expert, are "basically prototypes, with all the kinks and problems a prototype has." Except these prototypes, filled with lots of jet fuel, ferry actual people around.

The market opportunity for aircraft

in Russia is estimated to be $60 billion, or about 750 aircraft, over the next 20 years. For now the bulk of that deal volume with be gobbled up by Boeing and especially Airbus, which has sold 147 planes in Russia, 79 of them new, over the past 5 years. The Russian consortium's main contender to compete with the Airbus 320 and Boeing 757 will be the Irkut MS-21, though that's not due out until 2017. That will give us a glimpse as to whether Russia's domestic aircraft industry will ever get its sea legs back.

Between the legacy planes and the appalling pilot culture, though, the next few years promise to be bumpy. Just in the time between when I began writing this story and when I finished, an Airbus flying over the Siberian city of Kirov had to make a crash landing, its fuselage filled with smoke. Ⓕ

IT'S BETWEEN YOU AND THE SMOKY MOUNTAINS

E RACE ELIMINATION RUN SPARTAN RACE OBSTACLE COURSE UPHILL BIKE RACE UPHILL RUN OPEN WATER SWIM & KAY

ARE YOU THE FITTEST CEO®

SEPTEMBER 13-16, 2012

CEO WORLD CHAMPIONSHIP

BLACKBERRYFARM

For Reservations and More Information, 720-663-9335
or visit WWW.CEOCHALLENGES.COM for details!

Above: Front view of the first prototype A-40 on the runway at Taganrog. The outrigger floats have now been fitted. Note the triple black stripes across the tops of the outer wings (probably for photo calibration).

This rear view shows the nozzles of the booster turbojets in the rear ends of the main gear sponsons below the nozzles of the D-30KPV cruise turbofans. Oddly, the elevators are set at different angles.

Above: Another view of the first prototype parked on the runway (note the wheel chocks). The nozzle of the TA-12A APU under the port main gear sponson was originally flush with the skin as shown here.

This view shows the A-40's elegant lines and the inclined position of the main gear struts. No water rudder was fitted initially, and the cheatline and the decorative stripes on the engine nacelles were all plain blue.

Above: The first prototype A-40 becomes airborne at Taganrog in 1987. The nozzles of the booster jets are closed by eyelid shutters. Note the extended APU nozzle protruding from the sponson; also, the main door is now heavily outlined, and the cheatline and the nacelle stripes are edged in white.

A-40 '10 Red' taxies at Taganrog, with a Be-30 feederliner in the background. Note the addition of dielectric panels on both sides of the fin fillet.

This page, above left: This close-up of the A-40's forward fuselage shows such details as the radome's curvature and tension locks, the IFR probe and associated retractable drogue illumination lights to be used during night refuelling, the flightdeck roof escape hatch and the spray dam ahead of the windshield.

Above right: The main gear units have double-jointed 'knee-action' struts allowing them to fold into the smallest possible space. Note the bogie tilting ram/rocking damper ahead of the drag strut.

Right: The weapons bay located aft of the main step is closed by clamshell doors.

Opposite page, top: The first prototype A-40 flies above thick overcast with the landing gear extended during an early test flight, showing the no-load position of the main gear bogies with the front axle down. Note the wing stripes (later removed) and the extra spray deflectors on the centre fuselage.

Centre: The same aircraft at a later date, pictured seconds before becoming airborne from Ghelendjik Bay with all four engines running. Note the deployed flaps, the stabilisers set to maximum negative incidence and the extreme angle of attack immediately before lift-off. A blue 'arrow' has been added on the vertical tail.

Bottom: The first prototype about to alight on Taganrog Bay in 1987 during the opening stage of the seaworthiness tests. There is still no water rudder.

Above left, the second prototype's port flap and open weapons bay doors flanked by hydrodynamic deflectors; right, the water rudder and the rear antenna fairings of the mission avionics suite.

Above: The second prototype's port main gear sponson and engine pylon carrying the port D-30KPV cruise engine and the port RD36-35 take-off booster with the nozzle 'eyelids' closed.

The outrigger floats are mounted on short pylons, with ECM pods at the latter's junction with the wingtips.

with a hose-and-drogue IFR system, the IFR probe being located on top of the forward fuselage. The rear part of the hull hosed a weapons bay 6.1 m (20 ft) long.

To improve field performance and ensure safety in the event of an engine failure the designers decided to use a mixed powerplant on the A-40. It comprised two 12,000-kgp (26,455-lbst) Solov'yov D-30KPV turbofans augmented by two 2,350-kgp (5,180-lbst) Kolesov RD36-35 turbojets. The D-30KPV was a version of the familiar D-30KP (powering the IL-76) with enhanced corrosion protection and no thrust reverser. The cruise engines were located in pylon-mounted nacelles above the main gear fairings so that the air intakes were shielded by the wings, while the take-off booster turbojets were buried in the aft ends of these fairings, breathing through intakes closed by doors; the nozzles were closed by vertically split eyelid shutters. This engine placement protected them from water spray ingestion during take-off and alighting.

Now that the basic configuration and the main structural and layout features of the new amphibian had been determined, a government decision was required calling for full-scale development and prototype construction.

Much time elapsed before Chief Designer A. K. Konstantinov finally succeeded in 'legalising' the work on the Albatross through negotiations first with the then Minister of Aircraft Industry Pyotr V. Dement'yev and then with his successor V. A. Kazakov. In April 1980 the CofM Presidium's Commission on defence industry matters (VPK – *Voyenno-promyshlennaya komissiya*) issued a special ruling calling for the development of the A-40 amphibian, followed on 12th May 1982 by

Council of Ministers No.407-111 to the same effect. Ghennadiy S. Panatov became project designer, and a year later he was promoted to Deputy Chief Designer with special responsibility for this aircraft.

Once the project had been 'legalised', detail design and the manufacture of a full-scale mock-up could begin, proceeding at full speed and accompanied by preparations for prototype construction. The CofM directive stipulated that two flying prototypes (articles 'V1' and 'V2') and one static test airframe (article 'SI' – that is, *staticheskiye ispytahniya*) were to be built at the OKB's prototype construction facility with assistance from TMZD (N. N. Ozherel'yev was the plant's director at the time). The manufacturing drawings were transferred to the workshops in 1983, and the first machine was laid down into the jig in June of the same year.

The hull and the wings were manufactured of large panels; many parts of complex shape were milled from a single half-finished article. The neighbouring TMZD plant manufactured large assemblies – the wing centre section, outer wing panels (with high-lift devices and systems), and the stabiliser. Then they were delivered to the OKB's experimental production facility for final assembly. The officially endorsed programme schedule and construction schedule were revised several times. One reason for this was the high labour intensity of the new machine; also, production assets were frequently diverted to other equally important assignments.

In parallel with the construction of the first prototype a vast programme to develop and verify the aircraft's key design and layout features was performed on testbeds, stands and rigs. Several dozen test facilities were built within the A-40 programme for the purpose of

Above: The flightdeck of the first prototype A-40. The round box on the captain's control wheel houses a turn angle sensor which is part of the test equipment. The centre of the instrument panel is a bit bare.

checking out various aircraft systems and equipment. These facilities included a full-scale 'iron bird' rig for the control system, full-scale rigs for the electric system, fuel system, the Verba flight/navigation suite and the STS, and so on. The powerplant was also verified on a full-scale rig, which made it possible to test the engines on the ground in all modes, including the extinguishing of a real fire. Tests conducted on rigs and stands made it possible to minimise the technical risk, to save time during the development testing and to preclude various incidents on the aircraft during its operation.

Coded '10 Red', the first prototype was rolled out on 9th September 1986 after a traditional festive ceremony attended by numer-

ous employees of the TMZD plant and the OKB. Following the traditional rite, Aleksey K. Konstantinov broke a bottle of champagne against the towbar, and a tractor towed the first A40 to the hardstand of the flight test facility. There the A-40 was soon discovered by US intelligence satellites; since the manufacturer was unknown to the West at the time, the aircraft received the temporary reporting name *Tag-D* (the 'Tag' stood for Taganrog). Later, when the machine had been identified as a Beriyev product, it was aptly codenamed *Mermaid* by NATO.

Test pilot 1st Class Yevgeniy A. Lakhmostov was appointed project test pilot for the A-40; he was an experienced naval pilot who had previously flown the Be-6 flying

The first prototype in its definitive colour scheme is depicted here a second before touchdown. Note the addition of the water rudder.

Above: The Beriyev TANTK test crew that flew the A-40 on its record-breaking flights on 13th-14th September 1989.

programme included only runs with speeds up to and including rotation speed (involving actual rotation). After a pre-flight briefing the crew took their seats in the aircraft. The crew comprised captain Ye. A. Lakhmostov, co-pilot B. I. Lisak, navigator L. F. Kuznetsov, flight engineer V. A. Chebanov, radio operator L. V. Tverdokhleb and operator-engineer in charge N. N. Demonov. Meanwhile, Stepanov went to the control tower.

The day's test programme was largely completed during the first half of the day; the only thing remaining was a check of the elevator authority. One of the runway thresholds at the factory airfield in Taganrog was located right next to the shore of Taganrog Bay. The high-speed runs were performed in the direction away from the sea, but by noon the wind changed its direction, and the aircraft was towed to the opposite end of the runway.

During a run in the direction of the bay, at 15:59 Moscow time the aircraft lifted off unexpectedly; the remaining length of the runway was not sufficient for landing and a braking run, and Lakhmostov had no other option but to continue the take-off. Having made the first landing approach, Lakhmostov assessed the aircraft's controllability and made a go-around; then, at 16:16, the A-40 landed safely.

This is how Lakhmostov himself described what had happened: *'During the second run, with the control column pulled back, at a speed of 160-170 km/h [99-106 mph] the aircraft pitched up briskly. When I throttled back and pushed the control column forwards, in accordance with the test mission, this coincided with the aircraft lifting off the runway and gaining a height of 7-9 m [23-29 ft]. With the engines throttled back the aircraft was already flying at a speed of 200-210 km/h [124-130*

boat. N. N. Demonov was appointed engineer in charge of the testing.

On 7th December 1986 the first prototype (*izdeliye* V1) began taxiing tests and high-speed runs. Driven by curiosity, many employees of the plant hung around in the hope of witnessing the first flight of the new amphibian, but workshop foremen sent them back to their work places, giving them official assurance that nothing of the sort had been planned for the day. The taxi runs continued well into the afternoon until a thick fog enveloped the airfield, calling a halt to the work. Having discussed the results of the day's work with Lakhmostov, Aleksey K. Konstantinov flew to Moscow to arrange a meeting of a flight test procedures council; the latter was to discuss preparations for the A-40's maiden flight. Current affairs were left in the charge of the Chief Designer's first deputy A. N. Stepanov.

On the following day, 8th December, the tests continued. In accordance with the manufacturer's flight test plan, the day's

Kicking up spray with its engine efflux, the second prototype A-40 ('20 Red') comes out onto the slipway at Ghelendjik during Hydro Aviation Show-98 in July 1998 (note the Russian flag on the tail).

mph] *and, contrary to what I was accustomed to, showed no tendency to lose height. I was in doubt as to whether it would be safe to abort the take off (with regard to the remaining runway length); therefore I took a decision to continue the take-off, performed two circuits in the course of 17 minutes and made a landing'.*

The inadvertent take-off of the A-40 was due to a combination of several factors. These included the aircraft's good acceleration characteristics which were not duly taken into account by the crew, as well as the fact that the high-set thrust line caused the machine to raise its nose when the engines were throttled back.

The post-war history of Soviet aviation had already recorded cases when prototype aircraft took to the air against the will of the pilot. In September 1955 test pilot A. G. Kochetkov unintentionally took off in the Sukhoi S-1 fighter (the first prototype of the Su-7); showing presence of mind, he managed to perform a safe landing and was awarded the Order of the Red Star for his skill. Test pilot K. V. Chernobrovkin was less lucky, losing his life on 24th December 1978 in similar circumstances when testing the Myasishchev M-17 high-altitude aircraft. Lakhmostov on the A-40 became the third pilot who found himself in a situation like this. Albeit luckily completed, his flight exposed Konstantinov to protracted investigations in the Ministry of Aircraft Industry. As for Lakhmostov himself, despite the well-known maxim 'the victors are not judged' he was dealt with in a hard-handed manner. He was forced out of his job as a pilot and into retirement (but still did not give up flying!). He was succeeded by G. G. Kalyuzhnyy as the A-40's project test pilot.

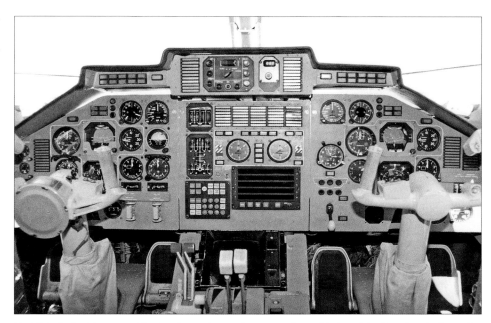

The flightdeck of the second A-40 makes an interesting comparison with that of the first aircraft pictured on page 59.

The second flight of the Albatross (also ranking as the first official flight) brought no particular surprises and took place in April 1987. After that the flight testing assumed its usual course.

The summer of 1987 saw the beginning of the water phase of the A-40's testing in Taganrog. On 27th July the amphibian was waterborne for the first time, and in August the first runs were started in Taganrog Bay. They revealed a slight longitudinal oscillation of the machine at speeds approaching the unstick speed; this was attributed to the aerofoil (or rather hydrofoil) effect of the shoals of the Azov Sea and did not cause any particular anxiety. The first take-off from water took place on 4th November 1987 (with a crew captained by G. G. Kalyuzhnyy); it revealed the A-40's longitudinal instability on take-off and, particularly, during the alighting. The surmise about the hydrofoil effect of the shoal was abandoned after conducting runs in a deep-water area of the Azov Sea. Flights from water were suspended; this coincided with the Taganrog Bay freezing up and thus provoked no particular enquiries from Moscow.

The test flights continued from the factory airfield; in the meantime, Beriyev OKB specialists (V. G. Zdanevich, V. N. Kravtsov, A. F. Shul'ga) and TsAGI specialists (G. V. Logvinovich, V. P. Sokolyanskiy, Yu. M. Ban'shchikov, V. A. Lukashevskiy)

The second prototype leaves the slipway, about to commence a demonstration flight at the 1998 Hydro Aviation Show; the landing gear is still down and is churning up the water. Note the different cheatline and the white-outlined 'arrows' on the tail and the engine nacelles.

Above: The second prototype A-40 in its original colour scheme climbs away at the beginning of a test flight. The landing gear is just completing its retraction sequence.

Left: Sand bags were used as the payload during the A-40's record-breaking flights on 3rd July 1998. Right: The crew leaves the aircraft after setting a time-to-height record.

tried to find an urgent solution of the problem thus posed. It was *déjà vu* – the problem that had arisen with the first jet-powered flying boat, the R-1, was seemingly repeating itself. Time passed, yet numerous experiments with A-40 models in the TsAGI towing tank brought no positive results. The solution was found as a result of more thorough studies of the water flow behind the hull step. The character of the flow differed substantially from the usual pattern in the case of an unflared V-bottom. V. G. Zdanevich and V. N. Kravtsov suggested that special deflectors be mounted on the planing bottom aft of the step. The very first tests confirmed the soundness of the idea. The amphibian's hydrodynamic instability problem was solved. Further work on the hydrodynamics of the planing bottom conducted by specialists of TsAGI and the OKB led to the definitive configuration that was adopted for the aircraft. Interestingly, subsequent research on choosing the optimum location for the deflectors showed that the best solution was the first one, selected by sheer intuition.

Flights from water resumed in the spring of 1988. The modified A-40 displayed stable hydroplaning within the entire range of speeds. Thus, the Taganrog designers had produced an amphibian aircraft on a top-notch technical level. The OKB's specialists incorporated a great number of technical features ranking as inventions into its design, and nearly 60 international patents were issued for these.

In August 1989 the A-40 had its public debut at that year's Aviation Day display at Moscow-Tushino. Piloted by a crew captained by B. I. Lisak, the amphibian concluded the flypast of several new Soviet aircraft; it was presented to the general public as a prototype of a SAR amphibian (subsequently, this 'cover story' was to be repeated more than once). The demonstration of the new seaplane did not pass unnoticed, provoking much comment in the aeronautical press abroad. Of course, foreign specialists were not misled by the official explanations concerning the aircraft's mission, and in all foreign publications and comments the Albatross was referred to as a new ASW and maritime reconnaissance aircraft.

When the machine came back from Zhukovskiy, the testing resumed. To give a convincing proof of the aircraft's unique performance, it was decided to perform on it a number of record flights. On 13th and 14th September 1989 a crew comprising captain B. I. Lisak, co-pilot Konstantin V. Babich, navigator M. G. Andreyev, flight engineer V. A. Chebanov, radio operator L. V. Tverdokhleb and systems operator A. D. Sokolov set the A-40's first 14 world records in the classes of seaplanes and amphibian aircraft

Above and below: A-40 '20 Red' performs at the Hydro Aviation Show-98 in Ghelendjik.

The second prototype in an earlier guise as '378 Red' in the mid-1990s; the 'tactical code' was really the Paris exhibit code. Note the open APU air intake.

with regard to the altitude attained with a cargo and without a cargo.

In late 1989 the second A-40 prototype (*izdeliye* V2) coded '20 Red' joined the test programme; this aircraft was manufactured by the prototype construction facility on 30th November 1989. Sea trials of the first machine continued in the winter of 1988-89 when the amphibian was ferried from Taganrog to the

OKB's flight test and experimental water facility in Ghelendjik. Since A. K. Konstantinov could not reside permanently in Ghelendjik, he appointed his deputy Ghennadiy S. Panatov (who, as we remember, had special responsibility for the A-40 programme) as chief of the work conducted at the Ghelendjik facility. Seaworthiness testing of the Albatross showed the machine to have a high degree of

Above: '378 Red' takes off on a demonstration flight at the Hydro Aviation Show-96 in Ghelendjik in September 1996, already wearing the Russian flag on the tail instead of the red star.

Above: French President François Mitterrand examines a model of the A-40 at the 1991 Paris Air Show as Beriyev TANTK engineers explain the aircraft's key features to him.

reliability and stability; on one occasion the amphibian weathered a gale with waves 3.0-3.5 m (9ft 10 in-11ft 6in) high and wind speeds of 15-18 m/sec (30-36 kts), staying afloat.

In the following year the testing went on with the participation of two machines. Right in the middle of the manufacturer's flight test programme, the Beriyev firm had a change of leadership. A. K. Konstantinov retired from his post of Chief Designer and was succeeded by G. S. Panatov. Hence in 1991 A. P. Shinkarenko became project designer of the A-40.

In the same year the A-40 was demonstrated abroad for the first time (the sensitive mission equipment, including the telescopic MAD boom, was deleted, and the machine was again presented as an SAR aircraft with the spurious designation A-42). This demonstration took place on 13th-23rd June 1991 at the 39th Paris Air Show held at Le Bourget where the second prototype was shown both statically and in flight; G. G. Kalyuzhnyy was

The A-40 commences its take-off run at the Air Expo '92 in Auckland, New Zealand.

the captain. For the occasion the original tactical code '20 Red' was changed to '378 Red' – actually an exhibit code.

The A-40 became one of the main show-stoppers at Le Bourget. Suffice it to say that the A-40 was the only aircraft which was boarded by the then President of France François Mitterrand when he examined the exhibits in the show. All aeronautical publications dealing with the Paris Air Show carried photographs of the Albatross and features or items devoted to it, in which they noted the perfection of the aircraft's elegant contours and assessed its performance highly.

Confirming the high appraisals accorded to it in France, on 19th, 22nd and 23rd July 1991 the A-40 established another series of world records. The aircraft was piloted by crews captained by G. G. Kalyuzhnyy and V. P. Dem'yanovskiy.

On 17th August 1991 the A-40, again captained by Kalyuzhnyy, took part in an air show which was held at Kiev-Gostomel', the flight test facility of the Antonov ANTK. In November of the same year the A-40 was filmed, along with the Be-12, by a French TV crew of the TF1 TV channel who came to the Soviet Union for the purpose of shooting a popular science film on seaplanes. Subsequently the film ran on Eurovision and was a success, while this

work itself became the first foreign contract for the Beriyev TANTK.

The end of the year and the beginning of 1992 brought more world records. The flights were performed on 19th and 21st November 1991 (with K. V. Babich and B. I. Lisak as captains) and on 26th March 1992 (captains Kalyuzhnyy and Dem'yanovskiy).

In February-March 1992 the second prototype (with a crew captained by Kalyuzhnyy) made a flight along the Taganrog - Tashkent - Calcutta - Singapore route. The purpose was to participate in the Asian Aerospace '92 air show in Singapore.

From 11th to 16th August 1992 Russian journalists and the public at large were able to examine the A-40 at close quarters when '378 Red' was in the static park of MosAeroShow '92, Russia's first real international airshow, at Zhukovskiy.

In November 1992 the Air Expo '92 international aeronautical exhibition was held in Auckland, New Zealand; the Beriyev TANTK received an invitation to take part in the exhibition. Again it was the second prototype A-40 that came to represent the company in the southern hemisphere. The flight to New Zealand and back along the Taganrog - Dubai - Colombo - Jakarta - Perth - Sydney - Auckland route, with a total one-way distance of

18,620 km (11,572 miles), became in itself a good test for the aircraft. The flight proceeded in adverse weather conditions: rain, thunderstorms and a hailstorm were encountered en route. Test pilots noted that even when the aircraft had to enter powerful cumulus clouds, it retained excellent handling. The Taganrog - Dubai leg of the journey passed over land, the rest of the route above the ocean. Nevertheless, the crew captained by Kalyuzhnyy successfully covered this route in a total of 28 hours 20 minutes' flight time.

As was the case in Paris, in Auckland the amphibian riveted everybody's attention. Every day numerous visitors wishing to come aboard queued up near the Albatross. A journalist responsible for one of the popular features on a local TV channel saw his ratings skyrocket after the channel had shown live a rite of his consecration to the rank of a naval pilot after a flight on the A-40. The rite included the drinking of a glass of a 'liquid containing alcohol' with the subsequent dipping of the 'consecrated' into water that was fairly cold by local standards – something like +18°C (64°F). The visitors to the show took much interest in a display stand telling the story of the Beriyev TANTK and of seaplane construction in Russia at large.

A fine air-to-air study of the Albatross, showing the high-aspect-ratio wings.

Between 31st August and 5th September 1993 the A-40, together with the Be-12P fire-bomber and the Be-32 feederliner, was among the exhibits of the MAKS-93 international aerospace show in Zhukovskiy. This time the amphibian also took part in the flying display.

During the period of Mikhail S. Gorbachov's *perestroika* (restructuring) and *glasnost'* (openness) the Albatross attracted interest even from the former 'potential adversaries' turned 'potential friends', including Great Britain. In 1992-93 the Royal Navy looked into the possibility of replacing the land-based British Aerospace Nimrod MR.2 maritime patrol aircraft with A-40s. The Beriyev TANTK looked into the possibility of fitting the amphibian with avionics and weapon systems similar to those of the Lockheed P-3C Orion and with Western engines. A programme to build such a 'Westernised' version of the A-40 was presented by TANTK General Designer G. S. Panatov at a meeting of the NATO Naval Armaments Group in Bruxelles in March 1993; it was given wide coverage by the Russian media which, with typical wishful thinking, even managed to 'sign' a contract for the delivery of such aircraft several times! Yet, the matter did not progress further than the stage of proposals and good intentions (with which the proverbial road is paved).

Nevertheless, the Albatross did set its foot in Britain, so to speak, when '378 Red' was demonstrated at an airshow in Woodford on 23rd-28th June 1993; as a souvenir from that event the aircraft received a bright conspicuous badge plastered on its side. The Russian pilots – Magomed O. Tolboyev flying a Sukhoi Su-27 fighter and a crew captained by G. G. Kalyuzhnyy on the A-40 – had the distinction of being the first to open the flying

Specifications of the A-40

Engines	2 x D-30KPV turbofans + 2 x RD36-35 turbojets
Thrust, kgp (lbst)	2 x 15,000 (2 x 38,075)
Length overall	43.84 m (143 ft 10 in)
Height on ground	11.0 m (36 ft 1 in)
Wing span	41.62 m (136 ft 6 in)
Wing area, m² (sq ft)	200.0 (2,153)
Maximum all-up weight, kg (lb)	86,000 (189,630)
Maximum speed, km/h (mph)	800 (497)
Take-off run (land/water), m (ft)	1,000/2000 (3,280/6,560)
Landing/alighting run, m (ft)	700/900 (3,300/2,950)
Seaworthiness (height of wind-induced wave), m (ft)	Up to 2.0 (6.5)
Crew	8

display in adverse weather on the final day of the show (on that day the cloudbase was as low as 200 m (660 ft) and it was raining). Getting ahead of our story, we may say that the second prototype Albatross visited Britain again in 1996. On that occasion the machine took part in the Royal International Air Tattoo '96 airshow that took place at RAF Fairford, Gloucestershire, from 17th to 22nd July.

By 1994 the flight development test programme had been completed, and the aircraft was in the middle of its state acceptance trials programme. In the course of these, between August 1990 and March 1991, a part of the aircraft's STS was tested at the Navy's test range in Feodosiya on the Crimea Peninsula. Normally during tests of such a large and complex aircraft the positioning flight to the Crimea was followed by preparations *in situ* lasting a couple of months. The Albatross, however, started the tests after a mere week. Proceeding from the test results, a decision was taken to start preparations for series manufacture, and a group of Air Force test

pilots mastered the piloting of the A-40. Plans were in hand for conducting comprehensive tests of the aircraft's STS against a real submarine target in 1993. A test range was prepared for this purpose, a vessel for experiments and a submarine were assigned to the programme; however, this work was suspended due to lack of funding.

A production batch of A-40s was to be manufactured at the Taganrog aircraft production association named after G. Dimitrov (formerly TMZD). A full set of technical drawings and other production documents had been transferred to the plant as early as 1986. New workshops had been built for the series production of the Albatross, jigs and other equipment had been manufactured, yet, construction of the pre-series batch of the A-40 never started because, in the turmoil that followed the break-up of the Soviet Union, state funding for the defence industry dried up.

Despite the cessation of funding for the A-40 programme, the second prototype became an unfailing participant of all hydro aviation shows that were held in 1996, 1998, 2000 and 2002 on the territory of the Beriyev TANTK's Ghelendjik test and experimental facility and of Ghelendjik airport.

While taking part in the Ghelendjik-98 air show, the second prototype A-40 demonstrated once again its unique capabilities by setting 12 new world records for seaplanes and amphibians in two flights on 3rd July; these were time-to-altitude records in which the aircraft climbed to 3,000; 6,000; and 9,000 m (9,840; 19,680; and 29,520 ft) with a payload of 15,000 kg (38,075 lb). Thus, the number of records set by the A-40 reached 140. In the first flight the aircraft was captained by Merited Test Pilot of Russia G. G. Kalyuzhnyy, in the second flight Colonel G. A. Parshin was in the captain's seat.

A-40M ASW Amphibian Aircraft (Project)

Upgrading the baseline ASW version, the military planned to equip the Albatross with a

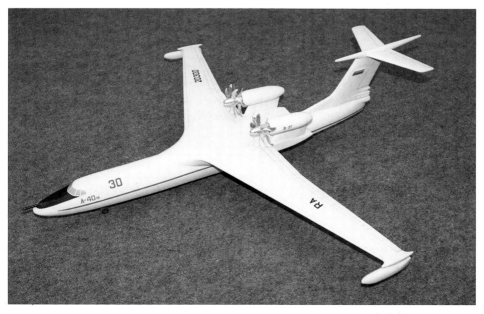

A model of the projected A-40M, showing the D-27 propfans on single pylons. Note the MAD boom at the top of the fin and the tail cannon barbette with associated radar.

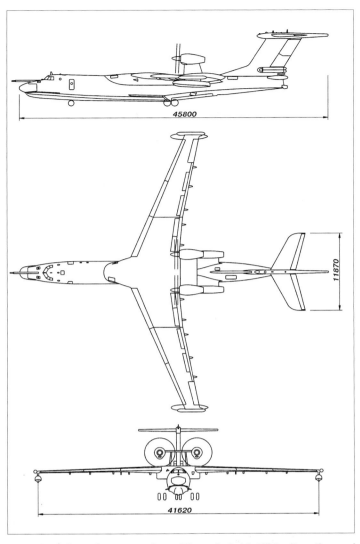 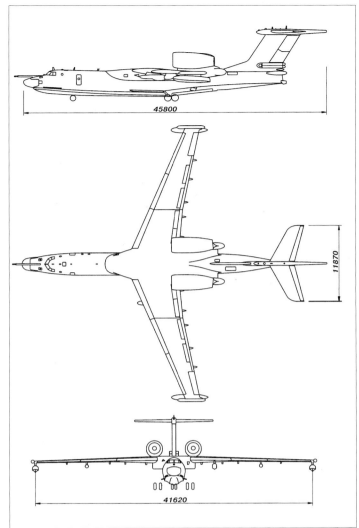

These three-views give a comparison of the projected A-40P in alternative versions with D-27 propfans (left) and PS-90A turbofans (right) as the cruise engines. Note that in this case the D-27 propfans are mounted at the ends of a horizontal airfoil structure supported by twin pylons and resembling the Greek letter 'pi'.

new search and targeting system (STS). The A-40 version with the new system was to be designated A-40M (*modernizeerovannyy* – updated). However, since series production of the A-40 never started, the A-40M version remained a paper project. Interestingly, a model of the A-40M was exhibited in a version powered not by turbofans but by 14,000-ehp ZMKB Progress (Muravchenko) D-27 propfan engines driving Aerosila SV-27 tractor propfans; the engines were carried at the ends of a horizontal airfoil supported by twin pylons.

A-40P ASW Amphibian Aircraft (Project, second use of designation)

The demise of the A-40M project did not lead the Beriyev TANTK to abandon further studies aimed at the development of a new ASW seaplane because the need for it did not diminish. Now, however, the ASW version of the Albatross designated A-40P (*patrool'nyy* – patrol, used attributively) faced competition from the Tu-204P project. In the spring of 1994 Russia's Ministry of Defence called a

competition for a new ASW aircraft because it could afford only one programme. Within the framework of the competition the A-40P project was reworked to take D-27 propfans and featured a maximum possible degree of commonality with the A-42 SAR aircraft.

The aircraft was to be fitted with the *Sova* (Owl) STS featuring a radar antenna enclosed in the nose radome. The combat load, reaching a maximum of 6,500 kg (14,332 lb), would

comprise up to three *Orlan* (Sea Eagle) ASW torpedoes or up to six ASW guided missiles of the Korshun (Kite, the bird), Yastreb (Hawk) and *Oryol* (Eagle) types. Provision was made for the carriage of Kh-35 subsonic anti-shipping missiles under the wings. In addition to guided weapons, the Albatross would be able to carry the whole range of mines, bombs and torpedoes that were in the arsenals of the Russian Army.

Specification of the A-40P ASW Aircraft

Engine type and power/thrust rating, ehp/kgp (lbst)	D-27A	PS-90A
cruise engines	2 x 14,000 ehp	2 x 16,000 (2 x 35,280)
take-off boosters	n.a.	n.a.
Useful load, tonnes (lb)	4-9 (8,820-19,845)	4-9 (8,820-19,845)
Cruising speed, km/h (mph)	710 (441)	710 (441)
Base	1st class airfield water aerodrome	1st class airfield water aerodrome
Seaworthiness, wind force (wave height 2 m (6 ft 6 in)	4-5	4-5
Crew	7	7

Above: This artist's impression from the project documents shows the A-40P firebomber in action.

Specifications of the A-40P Firebomber

Length overall	42.28 m (138 ft 8½ in)
Height on ground	11.066 m (26 ft 3¾ in)
Wing span	41.62 m (136 ft 6 in)
Wing area, m² (sq ft)	200.0 (2153)
Maximum all-up weight, kg (lb)	90,000 (198,450)
Maximum useful load, kg (lb)	25,000 (55,125)
Cruise engines	2 x D-30KPV turbofans
Engine thrust, kgp (lbst)	2 x 12,000 (2 x 26,460)
Take-off booster engines	2 x RD-38K turbojets
Engine thrust, kgp (lbst)	2 x 2,985 (2 x 6,580)
Maximum speed, km/h (mph)	800 (497)
Cruising speed, km/h (mph)	750 (466)
Length of water strip required for operation, m (ft)	3,200 (10,500)
Endurance, hours	10
Seaworthiness (height of wind-induced wave), m (ft)	Up to 1.5 (5)
Crew	5

The management of the Beriyev TANTK was doing its best to turn the situation around and secure funding for the A-40 development programme. As a part of this effort, steps were taken to get the then Minister of Defence, Army General Pavel S. Grachov, to visit the company. The visit took place from 31st May to 1st June 1995. The Minister familiarised himself with the state of affairs in the enterprise, listened to a report by General Designer Ghennadiy S. Panatov, and then was given a visit to the TANTK test facility and a ride on the second prototype A-40 followed by alighting on Ghelendjik Bay.

Summing up his impressions from the visit to TANTK, the Minister gave a highly favourable appraisal to the A-40, acknowledging the need for such an aircraft in the Russian Armed Forces, and called for work on the A-40 and A-40P to be included in the list of items for priority funding. At the same time Grachov suggested that one more version, a troopship variant of the amphibian, be developed. A project of this version was promptly prepared but, unfortunately, no real improvement in the funding for the purposes of either further testing or series production followed.

Despite the vast amount of scientific and technical research data accumulated over the years and the preparations for series manufacture that had been done, further work on this aircraft has not received due funding from the State. Thanks to their ability to perform its mission both in the air and when afloat, amphibian aircraft are more efficient than carrier-borne and land-based aircraft. Nevertheless, in 1995 the Ministry of Defence took a decision to put the research and development work on the A-40 on hold in favour of starting

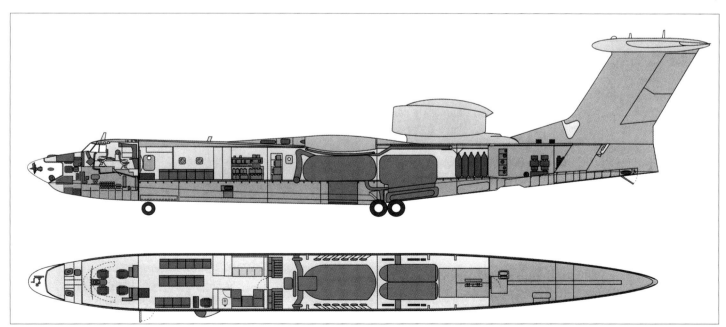

A cutaway drawing of the A-40P firebomber showing the water/fire retardant tanks, the cabin for fire-fighters at the front (featuring an observer's station) and the 'war room' aft of it.

the development of a new ASW aircraft – the Tu-204P, based on the Tu-204 medium-haul airliner that was already in production. The decision-makers proceeded from the assumption that the Tu-204P would have maximum commonality with the baseline passenger version, which was expected to be manufactured in large numbers, which promised a substantial reduction of operating costs. It seemed that the history of the A-40 thereby reached its end. However, the number of the Tu-204/Tu-214 aircraft manufactured in the recent years has reached a mere two dozen, and the Tu-204P project has been shelved as well.

In the meantime, ASW missions are again acquiring paramount importance in the range of tasks posed before the Russian Naval Aviation. The only difference is that previously priority was given to combating strategic missile-carrying submarines, while at present the multi-role submarines armed with cruise missiles for dealing strikes against coastal installations are the main targets. It was exactly the strikes delivered by sea-launched cruise missiles against anti-aircraft defences and control and communication centres that marked the beginning of all recent local wars.

The ASW version of the A-40 has been an object of constant interest on the part of a number of potential customers (China, India, Malaysia and others). An export version of the A-40 was developed for foreign customers; it featured the Sea Dragon STS incorporating a dunking sonar. The STS also includes a high-resolution thermal imaging system, a system of optical sensors and other equipment which enables the aircraft to detect and destroy both submarines and surface targets.

Specification of the A-40PM Passenger Amphibian

Length overall	42.10 m (138 ft 1³¹⁄₆₄ in)
Height on ground	11.00 m (36 ft 1 in)
Wing span	41.62 m (136 ft 6 in)
Wing area, m² (sq ft)	200.00 (2153)
Maximum all-up weight, kg (lb)	90,000 (198,450)
Maximum payload, kg (lb)	11,500 (25,357)
Maximum fuel load, kg (ft)	39,100 (86,215)
Powerplant	2 x CFM56-5C4
Engine thrust, kgp (lbst)	2 x 14,165 (2 x 31,230)
Maximum speed, km/h (mph)	730 (453)
Cruising speed, km/h (mph)	670 (416)
Take-off speed, km/h (mph)	250 (155)
Landing speed, km/h (mph)	180 (112)
Take-off distance (land/water), m (ft)	1,600/2,000 (5,250/6,560)
Landing distance (land/water), m (ft)	1,150/1,030 (3,772/3,027)
Service ceiling, m (ft)	10,000 (32,800)
Range with a maximum payload, km (miles)	5,000 (3,107)
Seaworthiness (height of wind-induced wave), m (ft)	Up to 1.5 (5)
Crew/passengers	2/121

A-40P Firebomber
(Project, first use of designation)

Over the years the Beriyev TANTK has considered developing various civil version of the A-40. Thus, back in 1991 the A-40P amphibian intended for putting out forest fires was brought out (in this case the P stood for *pozharnyy* – fire-fighting, used attributively). Water tanks with an appropriate venting system were installed in the centre fuselage (in the former weapons bay) and discharged through doors in the planing bottom; additionally, tanks for a chemical fire retardant would be housed in the equipment bay amidships. The aircraft was designed to scoop up 25 tonnes (55,125 lb)

of water by means of retractable scoops aft of the main step as it skimmed along the surface. In addition to water/fire retardant drops, the A-40P would cater for delivering teams of firemen and their equipment to the fire site (both by alighting on a suitable body of water nearby and by paradropping), for patrolling large forest areas with a team of fire-fighters on board (with an endurance of 9 to 10 hours) and for aerial photography of fire sites and the adjoining localities. The parachutists/fire-fighters would be accommodated in the cabin previously intended for the ASW equipment operators. A port side observation blister and a small 'conference room' were provided.

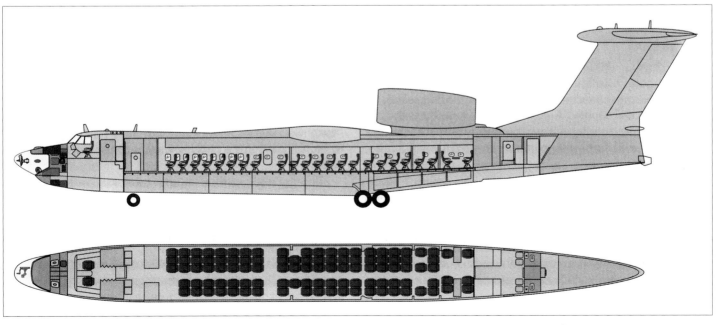

A cutaway drawing of the A-40PM amphibious airliner.

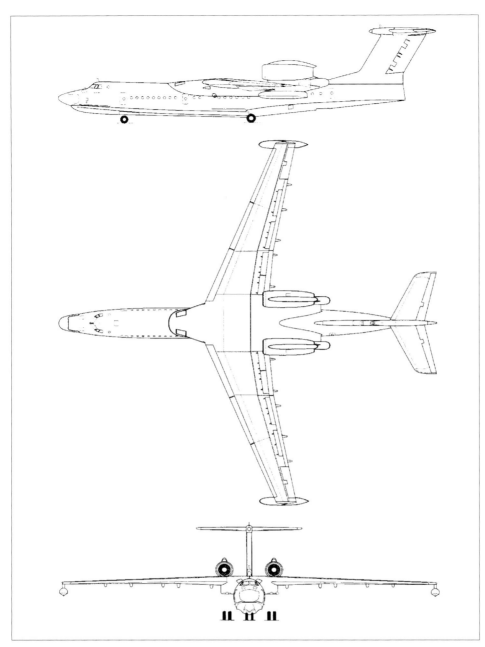

A-40PM (Be-40P) Passenger Amphibian (Project)

A passenger version of the A-40 designated A-40PM (some advertising booklets called it Be-40P for *passazheerskiy* – passenger, used attributively) and seating up to 121 passengers five-abreast was developed in 1994; it was intended for medium-haul routes in coastal areas where land airfields were scarce. In 105-seat configuration it could cover a distance of up to 4,000 km (2,486 miles). The passenger amphibian aircraft was projected in two versions; the baseline version retained the D-30KPV cruise engines and Kolesov RD-38 booster turbojets, and a version powered by CFM International CFM56-5C4 turbofans was offered for export. These versions did not progress further than the drawing board. It was decided to develop for civil uses a scaled-down analogue of the A-40; the work on it eventually resulted in the creation of the Be-200 multi-purpose amphibian described in the next chapter.

Be-40PT Cargo/Passenger Amphibian (Project)

A cargo/passenger version of the A-40 seaplane designated Be-40PT (*passazheer-skiy*/**trahns**portnyy* – passenger/cargo, used attributively) was designed to deliver 70 passengers or 37 passengers and a cargo of 6.5 tonnes (14,332 lb) over a distance of up to 4,200 km (2,610 miles). In the all-cargo version the aircraft would transport 10 tonnes over a distance of up to 4,200 km.

A-42 (Be-42) SAR Seaplane (*Izdeliye* VPS, Project); A-44 Patrol Seaplane (*Izdeliye* VPR, Project)

The only other version of the Albatross which progressed beyond the paper stage was a search-and-rescue version of the A-40. This version of the A-40 was to supersede the Be-12PS (Be-14) SAR seaplanes in service units. However, the usual course of design

Above: A three-view of the projected A-40PM (Be-40P) airliner. The twin-wheel main gear units are provisional.

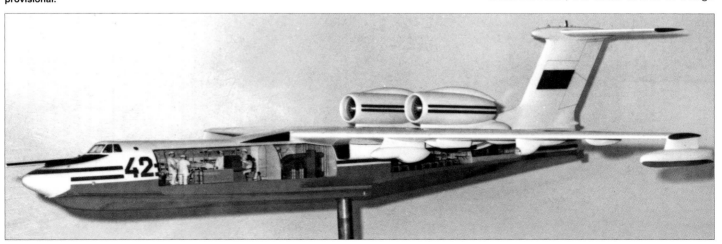

A cutaway display model of the A-42 (Be-42) SAR amphibian; interestingly, the aircraft is in civilian colours and lacks the wingtip ECM pods but still has IFR capability. The forward part of the cabin is a surgery room.

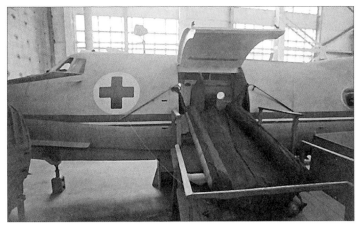 

Above: A full-scale mock-up of the A-42. The picture on the left shows the port side cargo door and the folding ramp facilitating the loading of stretcher cases.

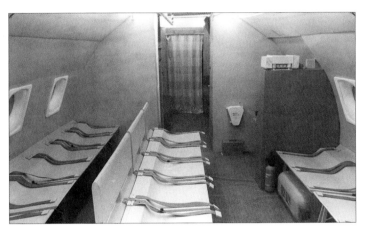 

Above left: The cabin for the walking wounded or rescuees featured tip-up seats of the sort fitted to military transports. Unlike the latter, seat belts were provided. The middle row tipped up against the supporting structure before it folded flush with the cabin floor for cargo carriage.
Above right: Four tiers of stretchers could be fixed to uprights in the cabin.

Above left: The surgery room allowing critically injured rescuees to be operated on en route to the hospital.
Above right: LPS-6 inflatable motor dinghies with a rigid bottom (seen here in deflated condition) were to be launched after alighting to pick up the rescuees.

work on the new SAR aircraft was affected by events having no direct connection with aviation.

On 7th April 1989 a tragedy occurred which stirred up practically the entire Soviet Union. A nuclear-powered submarine of the Northern Fleet – the K278 (SNS *Komsomolets*) – sank in the Sea of Norway; 42 of its crew died. A Northern Fleet Air Arm IL-38 ASW

aircraft participating in the SAR operation located the shipwrecked sailors, but all it could do was to drop life rafts and other survival equipment. After that, its crew, as well as the crew of a Norwegian P-3C Orion ASW aircraft, could only helplessly watch the tragedy that was unfolding beneath. The inflatable life rafts that had been dropped were deployed, but the wind blew them away from the dying

seamen. The crew of the submarine were freezing to death literally before everybody's eyes, and nobody could do anything.

These events had strong repercussions in the country. Among other things, they drew the attention of the Soviet Navy Command and the MAP top brass to the deficiencies of the An-12PS SAR aircraft (PS = *poiskovo-spasahtel'nyy* – search-and-rescue) equipped

Above left: The flightdeck of the A-42 mock-up with the pilots' seats slid all the way aft.
Above right: The flight engineer's workstation on the starboard side.

A display model of the A-42; the aircraft shares the basic grey colour scheme of its military progenitor but is registered RA-10725. The shape of the flightdeck glazing does not match the actual aircraft.

Specifications of the A-42 Amphibian

Engines	2 x D-30KPV turbofans + 2 x RD36-35 turbojets
Thrust, kgp (lbst)	2 x 15,000 (2 x 38,075)
Length overall	43.84 m (143 ft 10 in)
Height on ground	11.00 m (36 ft 1 in)
Wing span	41.62 m (136 ft 6 in)
Wing area, m² (sq ft)	200.0 (2,153)
Maximum all-up weight, kg (lb)	86,000 (189,630)
Maximum speed, km/h (mph)	800 (497)
Service ceiling, m (ft)	9,700 (31,825)
Take-off run (land/water), m (ft)	1,000/2,000 (3,280/6,560)
Landing/alighting run, m (ft)	700/900 (2,300/2,950)
Seaworthiness (height of wind-induced wave), m (ft)	up to 2.2 (7.2)
Crew (flight personnel/rescue workers)	5/4-5
Number of rescuees taken on board	53

with the air-droppable Yorsh (Ruff) boat and to the absence of a modern SAR amphibian capable of replacing the Be-12PS in Naval Aviation service. Chief Designer of the Beriyev TANTK Aleksey K. Konstantinov was urgently summoned to a session of a government commission held in Severomorsk to investigate the disaster. There he made a report on capabilities of the A-40 and the progress of work on the aircraft. Those present were impressed by the report, and VPK Chairman I. S. Belousov moved the development of a SAR version of the A-40 from the fourth to the first place in the list of priorities. In accordance with VPK ruling No.31 adopted in January 1990 the Beriyev TANTK was tasked with developing within the shortest time possible the A-42 (*izdeliye* VPS) SAR aircraft intended for SAR operations in the short- and medium-range zones of seas and oceans adjoining the territories of the Soviet Union. The same task called for the development of the A-44 (*izdeliye* VPR) maritime patrol version.

As can be seen from the project documents, the A-42 SAR version (in advertising booklets and exhibition materials it was often designated Be-42) differed from the ASW version in having large upward-opening side doors in the forward and rear parts of the boat hull (the forward door measuring 1.8 x 2.0 m/ 5 ft 11in x 6 ft 6 in) which made it possible to launch an inflatable motorboat with rescuers and pick up the persons in distress. To give urgent medical aid, a special compartment was fitted out as a surgery room provided with up-to-date equipment.

The medical team on board the aircraft would have at their disposal equipment for automatic monitoring of basic and more wide-ranging medical parameters, a blood transfusion apparatus for direct intravenous transfusion, devices for inhalation anaesthesia and artificial lung ventilation, an electrocardiograph, a set of medical aids for paradropping, a set of medicines for the treat-

high-lift devices. Their design incorporated an automatic system for the additional extension of the trailing-edge flaps, which were initially deflected to an intermediate setting and assumed the take-off setting only after the aircraft attained a high speed, when the spray jets became appreciably lower. The winglets envisaged originally were soon deleted. The airframe was manufactured mainly of aluminium alloys having enhanced corrosion resistance. Wide use was made of composite materials for a number of airframe units and parts, such as the leading-edge and trailing-edge sections of the wings, rudder, elevators, ailerons, flaps, spoilers, aft sections of the fin and stabiliser, water deflectors and floats.

A special 'maritime' corrosion-resistant version of the advanced fuel-efficient D-436 engine was urgently developed by the Ukrainian ZMKB Progress engine design bureau to power the Be-200; designated D-436TP, it was manufactured by the Motor Sich plant in Zaporozhye. The engine designers from Zaporozhye succeeded in tackling this task thanks to their 40-odd years of operational experience with the AI-20D Series III and IV turboprops on the Be-12 amphibian.

The new amphibian was to be equipped with modern avionics ensuring navigation and flight control under any weather conditions in any season, in daytime and at night. The ARIA-200 flight and navigation system was specially developed for the Be-200 as a joint effort by the Russian Avionics Research Institute (NIIAO – *Naoochno-issledovatel'skiy institoot aviatsionnovo oboroodovaniya*) and the American company Allied Signal Aerospace; it gave the aircraft ICAO Cat III blind landing capability. The system ensured navigation and flight control in adverse weather, as well as an automatic monitoring, diagnostics and recording of the functioning of onboard systems in flight and on the ground. All flight and systems information for the crew of two was presented on six full-colour liquid-crystal multi-function displays (MFDs) located on the instrument panel. Conventional electromechanical instruments were retained only as a back-up, should the electronics fail.

Much attention was paid by engineers designing the Be-200 to ensuring high manoeuvrability and good handling qualities, which were vital for a fire-fighting aircraft. Therefore the Be-200 became the first Beriyev aircraft to be equipped with fly-by-wire controls. The EDSU-200 triplex FBW control system (*elektrodistantsionnaya sistema oopravleniya*) was specially developed by the Moscow-based MNPK Avionika ('Avionics' Research & Production Complex); the flight-deck featured fighter-type control sticks instead of traditional control columns.

Furthermore, the Taganrog engineers had to tackle a multitude of design problems

Above: The still-unpainted first prototype Be-200 takes off from Irkutsk-2 airfield on its maiden flight on 24th September 1998.

when projecting the special fire-fighting equipment for the Be-200. Among other things, the testing of large scaled-strength models of seaplanes, full-scale seaplanes and amphibian aircraft showed that the highest stresses on the hull bottom, pitching oscillations, vertical travel of the CG and vertical G forces in the CG area arose during aquaplaning within the speed range between 60% and 85% of the unstick speed. On the other hand, if the water was scooped up into the tanks at speeds equal to 90-95% of the unstick speed, the amphibian stayed out of the zone of the highest stresses. This reduced fuel consumption and conserved engine and airframe service life. In addition, the time required for

Above: Already wearing a smart grey/red/blue colour scheme but still lacking a registration, the Be-200 was unveiled at Irkutsk-2 on 17th October 1998. Note the IAPO and Beriyev TANTK logos on the nose.

Three-quarters rear view of the first prototype, showing the separate core and bypass flow nozzles of the D-436TP engines.

Above, left and right: The cargo cabin of the first prototype Be-200 (RA-21511), looking aft. Test equipment racks are installed along the walls and the cabin trim is omitted for ease of access to the wiring and piping. Note the maintenance access hatches in the floor.

Left: The sliding 'top deck' access hatch at the aft end of the cabin and the associated ladder, looking towards the nose.
Right: The starboard side cargo door incorporates an inward-opening entry door.

Above left: The starboard engine nacelle. This engine placement, coupled with the ease of 'top deck' access, permits engine maintenance even when afloat.
Above right: The fin leading edge incorporates a water taxi light. The bulge on the fin fillet houses a ram air turbine providing emergency hydraulic power.

Above: Most of the Be-200's doors open forwards while remaining parallel to the fuselage side.
Right: The main gear units again have aft-inclined 'knee-action' struts. Unlike the A-40, the APU is on the starboard side. Note the spray deflectors ahead of the main step.

Left: The rear quartet of water discharge doors is located aft of the step, the outer pair featuring deflectors. Another four doors are located ahead of the step.
Right: Close-up of the water scoops located immediately aft of the main step, shown here in the retracted position.

taking on a load of water was reduced. These reasons contributed to the company's decision to develop a special system of fire-fighting equipment for the Be-200 that would allow the amphibian to scoop up water while skimming along the surface at 90-95% of the unstick speed.

This system was developed and put through its paces on a Be-12 amphibian (ex-Soviet Navy '46 Yellow', c/n 8601301) converted into a flying testbed. Registered RA-00046 after the conversion, it was designated Be-12P-200; the '-200' was a reference to the Be-200, distinguishing this particular

machine from the other Be-12P firebomber conversions (P = *pozharnyy* – fire-fighting). The work on modifying the aircraft proceeded under the direction of General Designer Ghennadiy S. Panatov and his first deputy A. V. Yavkin, with Yu. G. Dooritsyn as project designer. In addition to the development of

Above: The Be-200's planing bottom is flared at the front and features longitudinal strakes converging on the lower part of the radome. Note the forward pair of spray deflectors.

the water take-up and water discharge system for the new amphibian, the Be-12P-200 was used for developing techniques and methods of fighting forest fires.

After the break-up of the Soviet Union the Be-200 project was not closed down, unlike some other projects; moreover, the need for developing such an amphibian aircraft was confirmed by one more directive of the Government of the Russian Federation dated 17th July 1992. Yet, at the same time problems began to crop up with state funding and, as a consequence, with the choice of a production plant that would build the machine and with the manufacture of the numerous

outsourced components that were necessary. As G. S. Panatov aptly remarked, 'at that time everybody was busy counting money because nobody had it'.

In addition to Irkutsk, the Beriyev TANTK approached the aircraft plants in Kiev (KiGAZ 'Aviant', ex-plant No.473), Khar'kov (KhAPO, ex-plant No.135) and Omsk (OAPO, ex-plant No.166), offering the new amphibian as a potential product. Eventually, however, only IAPO displayed a cautious interest. Having thoroughly studied the machine under development and the methods to be used in its manufacture, the management of IAPO decided to go ahead with Be-200 production.

G. N. Gorbunov, the then General Director of IAPO, played a key role in this. He was the first to have faith in the Be-200; after carefully weighing all the pros and cons he firmly stated: 'We *shall* build the Taganrog amphibian!' An equally important role in the destiny of the Be-200 was played by V. A. Boguslayev, General Director of the Motor Sich company which was producing the D-436TP engine; this company offered Beriyev favourable financial terms.

Now, IAPO was predominantly a manufacturer of military aircraft, having built such types as the Antonov An-12A and An-24T transports, the Mikoyan MiG-23UB fighter trainer and MiG-27 strike aircraft; the Sukhoi Su-27UB trainer and Su-30 interceptor were its bread-and-butter product at the time. Since inviting direct investments from abroad into the enterprises of the Russian defence industry posed a lot of complications, a special joint-stock company known as BETAIR was set up for manufacturing and marketing the Be-200 (BETAIR is an acronym standing for **Be**riyev, **Ta**ganrog and **Ir**kutsk). In addition to TANTK, the venture had IAPO, ILTA-Trade Finances SA of Switzerland and the Industrial Investment Bank of the Ukraine as its participants. Valeriy A. Kobzev became General Director of the BETAIR JSC.

Construction of the first prototype Be-200 (c/n 7682000002; 768 is a code for the IAPO factory, 200 means Be-200 while the rest apparently means 0002nd airframe built) began at IAPO in 1992; the aircraft was built in the fire-fighting version. In order to speed up production entry it was decided to build the prototypes, making use of series production methods. As planned, the experimental batch comprised two flying prototypes and two airframes for static and fatigue tests.

The static test article (c/n 7682000001, *izdeliye* SI) and the fatigue test article (c/n 7682000004, *izdeliye* RI – *resoorsnyye ispytahniya*) were delivered from Irkutsk to Taganrog by a Russian Air Force An-124 in March 1995 and August 1997 respectively. The Be-200 was scheduled to fly as early as 1995; however, due to the general crisis of the Russian economy which inevitably affected the economic situation of the Beriyev TANTK and IAPO, it was not before the autumn of 1998 that the aircraft was prepared for the first flight. Test pilot Konstantin V. Babich was appointed project test pilot for the Be-200, with N. N. Demonov as project test engineer; Ye. V. Zarooba became the first technician of the prototype aircraft. During the flight testing the crew temporarily included a flight engineer whose workstation was outfitted in the cargo cabin.

The as-yet unpainted and unregistered first prototype of the Be-200 was rolled out on 11th September 1996. Specialists of the

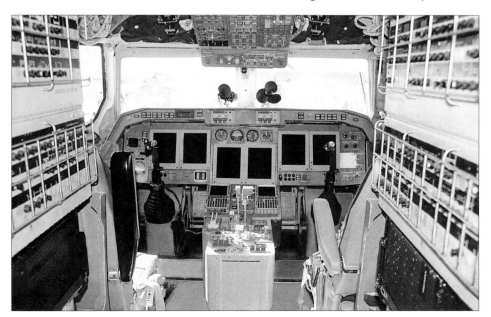

The flightdeck of RA-21511 had a provisional instrumentation fit. Among other things, the centre pair of MFDs was located lower than the others, with back-up electromechanical instruments above it.

Beriyev TANTK (headed by Be-200 project designer A. V. Yavkin) and IAPO worked around the clock, in three shifts, preparing the aircraft for its maiden flight. Despite the haste that characterised these preparations throughout, the session of the test flight procedures council passed without problems, and the Be-200 was cleared for the first flight.

It should be noted that operations from the IAPO airfield (Irkutsk-2) have their peculiarities. The problem is that the runway points towards a residential area. After the notorious crash of Russian Air Force An-124 '08 Black' (c/n 9773054516003) on 6th December 1997, when the aircraft hit several buildings outside the perimeter fence, killing many people on the ground, it was forbidden to perform take-offs in the direction of the residential blocks. But on the day of the first flight the weather was fine, with no wind; the wind started blowing after the aircraft had become airborne, but luckily in the 'right' direction.

The aircraft made its maiden flight from Irkutsk-2 airfield on 24th September 1998, piloted by a crew that comprised captain K. V. Babich, co-pilot V. P. Doobenskiy and flight engineer A. N. Ternovoy. The first flight lasted 27 minutes, with a Be-12P firebomber flying chase. Since the Be-200's approach speed is comparable to the Be-12's stalling speed, the chase aircraft had to resort to flying in an S-pattern over the runway in order to capture the Be-200's first landing on video.

Virtually the entire staff of the plant gathered to watch the first flight. Beriyev TANTK General Designer G. S. Panatov came to Irkutsk from Taganrog, in addition to the big group of specialists who helped prepare the machine for the maiden flight. Yevgeniy M. Primakov, the then Prime Minister of Russia, sent a telegram congratulating the staff of TANTK and IAPO with the first flight of the new aircraft on behalf of the Government.

On 29th September the machine made its second flight, which lasted an hour and a half. A third flight was planned for 30th September, but the weather turned bad, with wet snow falling, and the flight had to be cancelled even as the aircraft lined up for take-off. After that the tests were suspended, the Be-200 was rolled into a workshop for painting and routine maintenance. The flights resumed on 15th October, and an official presentation was held two days later. On that day the machine, now wearing a smart grey/red/blue colour scheme but still no registration, performed two demonstration flights for the benefit of the invited guests and journalists.

In the spring of 1999 the Be-200, by then finally registered RA-21511, was ferried to Taganrog for further testing. The flight on the Irkutsk-Novosibirsk-Ufa-Taganrog route was performed by a crew comprising captain K. V. Babich, co-pilot G. G. Kalyuzhnyy and navi-

The first prototype Be-200 waterborne at Ghelendjik during Hydro Aviation Show-2000 immediately after entering the water (top) and about to come ashore (above). The landing gear is still (or already) extended.

gator M. G. Andreyev. It was the 19th flight of the Be-200; by that time the amphibian had logged 26 hours 30 minutes.

Flight tests resumed in May; they included the first discharges of water onto the runway of the factory airfield. On 5th June the Be-200 performed a formation flight with the Be-12P-200 for the benefit of aerial photography and video filming. Four days later, wearing the exhibit code 368, the aircraft departed to Paris-Le Bourget for participation in the 43rd Paris Air Show. On the way to Paris (and back) the aircraft made an intermediate landing at Košice, Slovakia. At the show the Be-200 made a number of demonstration flights performed by the same crew (Babich, Kalyuzhnyy and Andreyev).

At the Paris Air Show the aircraft attracted immense interest on the part of specialists and the general public alike. It performed one training flight and two demonstration flights on 11th, 13th and 16th June, dropping 6 tonnes (13,230 lb) of water in each case. An amusing episode was associated with the firebombing demonstrations: when the airport authorities at Le Bourget received a request for this amount of water intended for filling the Be-200's tanks, the French were

quite surprised. Yet, with a truly Gallic sense of humour they suggested wine instead of water, because the price would be the same, and anyway they had no special vehicles for filling the aircraft's tanks with either of the two liquids. On 22nd June RA-21511 returned to Taganrog where preparations were started for the seaworthiness tests.

On 7th July the Be-200 'trod water' for the first time in order to check the sealing of the hull. The amphibian's first 'taste of the water' brought two nasty surprises. Firstly, the machine had a marked and stable tendency to bank to starboard; secondly, the hull proved to be rather leaky, shipping a fairly large amount of water. It became clear that the outrigger floats had insufficient displacement and were mounted on pylons that were of insufficient length; moreover, the starboard float was flooded to half its volume due to a leak in a bilge drain. As a remedy, the pylons were extended and the original floats were replaced with floats borrowed from the Be-12 to avoid delaying the test programme. Incidentally, these 'new' floats turned out to be 'oldies but goodies', proving to be well suited for the Be-200. The insufficient watertightness of the hull was also eliminated.

After these modifications the sea-going tests continued; on 6th and 7th August the aircraft performed its first high-speed water runs, reaching speeds up to 80% of the take-off speed. Although everybody wanted the machine to take to the air from water before the beginning of the MAKS-99 airshow in Zhukovskiy, General Designer G. S. Panatov wisely decided not to hurry. Tests on water were continued after the return of the aircraft from Zhukovskiy on 23rd August.

On 8th September 1999 the Be-200 prototype was demonstrated to Russia's Minister of Emergencies (= civil aid and protection) Sergey K. Shoigu who visited the Beriyev TANTK, accompanied by a group of specialists from his ministry. The Minister was advised on the progress of the flight test programme and held a conference on the introduction of the Be-200ChS (see below) into service with the Ministry of Emergency Situations (EMERCOM) and the subsequent operation of the aircraft. A decision was taken to create a training centre for hydro aviation specialists as a branch of the Beriyev TANTK where the flight and ground crews of seaplanes would receive their training. The Be-200 performed a demonstration flight, dropping a load of water on a simulated fire. The event was accompanied by the 'effect of the chiefs' presence', almost inevitable in such cases: the main gear units failed to retract due to a minor technical fault. True, this did not affect in any way the flight as such and the impression it produced on the guests.

On 9th September 1999 high-speed runs were again performed on the water virtually at unstick speed. According to captain Konstantin V. Babich, the machine behaved flawlessly and was ready to perform a take-off right away. Yet, the first flight from water was postponed until 10th September. The aircraft was put afloat around noon, but owing to a strong wind and rough seas in the bay the flight was delayed until the afternoon. At 17:45 Moscow time, when the weather had improved somewhat, the Be-200 multi-role amphibian made its first take-off from the water of Taganrog Bay. On this occasion the crew comprised captain K. V. Babich, co-pilot G. G. Kalyuzhnyy, navigator M. G. Andreyev and test equipment operator P. A. Lyashkov.

The flights from water resumed on 13th September; on 25th September test pilot N. N. Okhotnikov made a familiarisation flight as co-pilot. In all, by the end of October the amphibian had made some 80 test flights. In the following year of 2000 manufacturer's test flights and certification tests continued, interrupted from time to time by various demonstrations.

On 15th March 2000 the aircraft took part in a demonstration of the Russian aviation materiel intended for fighting forest fires; the demonstration was arranged for the EMERCOM top brass (headed by First deputy Minister Yu. L. Vorob'yov) and for representatives of potential foreign customers from Israel, Greece, Switzerland and France. The show took place on the territory of the factory air-

field and its water aerodrome. The Be-200 and Be-12P-200 amphibians demonstrated the take-up of water in aquaplaning mode, subsequently dumping the water on a simulated fire; the aircraft were captained by Babich and Okhotnikov respectively. In addition to the Beriyev TANTK aircraft, the participants of the show included EMERCOM's operational aircraft and helicopters; an IL-76TDP equipped with a VAP-2 water discharge device gave a water bombing demonstration, as did Mi-8MTV-1 and Mi-26T helicopters equipped with VSU-5 and VSU-15 'Bambi Bucket' underslung water discharge devices respectively. The choppers were able to replenish their water supply from the bay for a repeat demonstration.

On 8th November 2000 the A-40, Be-200 and Be-12P-200 amphibians from Taganrog took part in the demonstration of aviation materiel arranged for Russian President Vladimir V. Putin in Rostov-on-Don at the airfield of the Rostvertol enterprise. In all, by the end of the year the Be-200 had performed 153 flights and more than 50 water landings, including flights involving take-up and subsequent discharge of water.

Certification tests continued in 2001. The flights under the certification test programme were performed by Beriyev TANTK test pilots K. V. Babich, V. L. Fortushnov and N. P. Kuleshov, GosNII GA (State Research Institute of Civil Aviation) test pilot R. T. Yesoyan and LII (Gromov Flight Research Institute) test pilots A. I. Kostyuk and Yuriy P. Sheffer. In August 2001 the Be-200 reached an important milestone when it received a limited type certificate. From that moment on the amphibian could be used for real-life firefighting and training of flight crews for this aircraft could commence. At last, the Be-200 was turning from a prototype into a fully-fledged product suitable for export sales. By that moment the aircraft had performed a total of 223 flights within the framework of certification tests, logging 213 flight hours.

The type certificate was handed over to the General Designer under a festive ceremony during the MAKS-2001 airshow in Zhukovskiy on 15th August 2001. On the opening day of the show the Be-200 was inspected by President Vladimir V. Putin and Minister of Defence Sergey B. Ivanov who took much interest in the new machine and in the prospects of its potential use. During demonstration flights at the MAKS show the Be-200 performed spectacular discharges of water dyed in the colours of the Russian flag. The machine was piloted by a crew comprising crew captain K. V. Babich, co-pilot A. I. Kostyuk and navigator M. G. Andreyev. The aircraft returned from Zhukovskiy on 20th August, and as early as 21st and 22nd August the machine was flown for familiarisation pur-

The first prototype Be-200 taxies on the water of Taganrog Bay in September 1999; the port float is clear of the water. Note the exhibit code 368 with which the aircraft was displayed at that year's Paris Air Show.

poses from water and land by William Rice, chief pilot and vice-president of Liberty Airlines (USA).

On 23rd October 2001 the Be-200 multirole amphibian returned to Taganrog after successful appearances at the LIMA-2001 International Maritime and Aerospace Exhibition in Malaysia and the KADE-2001 Defence exhibition in South Korea. The overall length of the flight route was 22,391 km (13,916 miles), with intermediate landings in 14 cities of 8 countries. It was the first time the Be-200 performed such a long-distance flight.

The amphibian's grand Asian tour had started on 3rd October, when the machine piloted by a crew comprising captain K. V. Babich, co-pilot N. P. Kuleshov, navigator M. G. Andreyev and flight systems operator V. Ye. Zarooba lifted off the runway and took an eastbound course. The aircraft's route took it across Turkmenistan to the United Arab Emirates, and further over India and Myanmar to Malaysia where the LIMA-2001 show was to open at Langkawi Island a few days later.

The decision to choose Malaysia for demonstrating the Be-200 was not a matter of chance. LIMA is one of the most important military exhibitions in the Asian-Pacific region; it is attended by numerous real buyers of, and potential customers for, Russian aviation materiel – such as India, China, Malaysia, Philippines, Vietnam and Singapore. Furthermore, it was exactly the South-East Asia countries that displayed the greatest interest for the new amphibian aircraft. To top it all, this exhibition gave a chance to show the Be-200 in all its splendour – that is to say, on the water, because LIMA was from conceived the outset as a place for showing both aerospace technology and naval technology (at Site A and Site N respectively).

When the then Malaysian Prime Minister Dr. Mahathir Mohammad was inspecting the naval part of the exhibition, the Be-200 put up a brilliant show of scooping up water in aquaplaning mode, followed by a discharge of the water near the line-up of warships participating in the exhibition. The amphibian from Taganrog became one of the stars of the show, and its demonstration flights involving water bombing attracted much interest on the part of specialists and ordinary visitors alike. During the show, negotiations were held with official delegations from the Philippines, Indonesia, Singapore and Thailand. The Malaysian Minister of the Interior, whose ministry was responsible for forest fire protection among other things, paid special attention to the Beriyev display stand and to the new amphibian. The Minister's subordinates – the pilots of the air element of the fire-fighting service (BOMBA) who flew the fire-fighting missions – also examined the Be-200 at great

Above: The Be-200 poses for the camera as it flies low over the coastline of Taganrog Bay. The machine makes a very distinctive shape.

A water bombing demonstration by the Be-200 invariably wows the spectators; after all, this relatively compact aircraft can deliver six tons (13,230 lb) of water in one pass.

length. On the other hand, the deputy commander of the Royal Malaysian Air Force was interested in the prospects of operating future maritime patrol/SAR and transport versions of the Be-200.

The days spent at Langkawi passed quickly, and on 12th October RA-21511 set off on its further course to the Far East, taking the ground support crew with it. Passing over China and Vietnam, it headed for the next destination, Seoul – the capital of the Republic of Korea. There the aircraft took part in the Korean Aerospace and Defence Exhibition (KADE) held on 14th-19th October, performing demonstration flights in Korean skies just as brilliantly and successfully as it had in Malaysia. In the course of the Korean exhibition, too, fruitful negotiations were held with representatives of maritime police and of the ministry of forestry. It should be noted that the Beriyev TANTK had already established business ties with the well-known company LG, whose aviation subdivision is doing its best

for promoting the Be-200 on the South Korean market in fire-fighting and patrol versions.

On 20th October, having flown across China over the Yellow Sea and the Gobi Desert, the Be-200 finally crossed the Russian border. Further stops were made in Irkutsk, Novosibirsk, Ufa and, finally, the machine finished its round-the-world trip in Taganrog. This journey became a good test for the new aircraft, its engines and systems and, of course, its crew who had spent nearly 50 hours in the air.

Long-distance flights undertaken by the Be-200 were not limited to South-East Asia. On 8th May 2002 RA-21511 flew from Taganrog to Berlin-Schönefeld for participation in the ILA-2002 International Aerospace Show. Already on the following day the amphibian from Taganrog demonstrated its most spectacular show item – the discharge of water dyed in Russian flag colours – in the skies of Berlin. During the ILA show a memorandum

Above and below: The Be-200 demonstrates its ability to take on and offload cargoes while afloat, using an overhead hoist with an extensible rail. Note the cargo door opening angle and the twin actuators.

where a presentation took place at the Hellenic Air Force's Elefsis AB in the suburbs of Athens. This was followed by demonstration flights with the extinguishing of a simulated fire; Greek pilots were aboard the aircraft during these flights.

In all, the Be-200 prototype covered a distance of more than 7,600 km (4,720 miles) across Europe, performing 15 demonstration flights from land and eight flights from water. During this expedition (which was, in effect, a kind of service test) the aircraft was flown by a crew comprising captain K. V. Babich, co-pilot N. P. Kuznetsov and navigator M. G. Andreyev.

The reliability of the Taganrog amphibian and its ability to operate under most difficult conditions was corroborated once more by a series of test flights conducted in Armenia in August 2002. The purpose of the tests was to determine performance figures and evaluate the operation of the aircraft's equipment in extreme hot-and-high conditions. In Armenia the Be-200 took off and landed at Pomri airfield with an elevation of 1,580 m (5,180 ft) above sea level and on Lake Sevan situated in high mountains (1,950 m/6,400 ft ASL). At Sevan the aircraft took up and dropped water and performed single-engine take-offs, simulating an engine failure. It should be noted that flights of this kind were performed by an amphibian aircraft of this class for the first time in world practice. During these tests (in the course of which a total of some 25 hours was logged) the amphibian operated from Yerevan-Erebuni airport. It was piloted by a crew comprising captain K. V. Babich, co-pilot R. T. Yesoyan (an expert pilot from GosNII GA), navigator M. G. Andreyev, flight engineers S. A. Goondich and A. A. Kovalyov. By the end of August 2002 the first prototype Be-200 had logged more than 700 hours.

In September 2002, during the 4th International exhibition and scientific conference on hydroaviation in Ghelendjik (Hydro Aviation Show-2002), the Be-200 bettered its achievements established two years earlier in the same C-2 and C-3 classes. In one of the record flights, on 6th September, the role of co-pilot was performed by V. D. Morozov, Deputy C-in-C of the Russian Air Force for armament.

Be-200ChS Multi-Purpose Amphibian

The second prototype Be-200, RA-21512 (c/n 7682000003), took to the air at Irkutsk-2 airfield on 27th August 2002. During the 40-minute first flight it was piloted by a Beriyev test crew comprising pilots N. P. Kuleshov and N. N. Okhotnikov, as well as flight engineer A. N. Ternovoy. As distinct from the first prototype, it was built in the Be-200ChS version equipped to meet as fully as possible the requirements of the launch customer –

was signed between IAPO and the European Aviation, Defence and Space (EADS) consortium on co-operation in studying the market for the Be-200 amphibian. In particular, provision was made for studying jointly the scope of the market for the Be-200, preparing proposals on its international certification and the eventual establishment abroad of a post-sale maintenance system for the aircraft. Furthermore, negotiations were held with Rolls-Royce PLC on the possibility of fitting the Be-200 with Rolls-Royce turbofans for export.

After ILA-2002 the Be-200 performed demonstration flights in France and Greece in accordance with agreements concluded

earlier between EMERCOM of Russia and the civil aid and protection authorities of these two countries. On 13th May the amphibian flew from Berlin to Marseilles-Marignane airfield where it was shown to specialist of the *Securité Civile* (Civil Defence) board. In keeping with the request of the French side, the presentation included a demonstration of the Be-200's ability to scoop up water in aquaplaning mode and dump it on a (simulated) fire, as well as the loading and unloading of the standard equipment used by France's Civil Defence units.

Having concluded the French part of its European tour, the Be-200 flew to Greece

Above: RF-21515, the first production Be-200ChS, shows off the full livery of EMERCOM of Russia. Unlike the prototype, production examples have two unswept blade aerials on top of the fin instead of one.

Above: The second production example, RF-32516, has a slightly different colour scheme with no black anti-glare panel and no outline around the cargo door.

RF-32517, the third example delivered, at Zhukovskiy during the MAKS-2005 airshow. This machine has larger and more conspicuous EMERCOM 'windrose' logos.

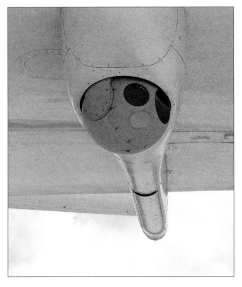

Above left: The cabin of Be-200ChS RF-32517 with generously spaced seats.
Above right: An optoelectronic observation system supplied by TAMAM is installed in a gyrostabilised 'ball turret' under the No.2 port flap track fairing.

Above left: The rear part of the cabin houses two inflatable life rafts supplied by the US company Air Cruisers. Note also the boarding ladder.
Above right: The port observation blister surrounded by a reinforcement plate. Note the supply tube of the alcohol de-icing system.

Left: The production Be-200ChS (illustrated by RF-32517) has an ARIA-200M EFIS with all six multi-function displays located in line.
Right: The observation system operator's workstation with a joystick controlling the 'ball turret'.

toilet for the crew and a galley up front (to port and starboard respectively), followed by a VIP cabin (with two armchairs and a table to port and a three-seat sofa to starboard that could be transformed into a bed), a cabin for guests of honour (with three forward-facing first class seats to port at 914 mm/36" pitch and a three-seat sofa to starboard), a cabin for the retinue with five rows of economy-class seats four-abreast at 812 mm/32" pitch, a wardrobe and hand luggage stowage further aft. The aircraft was equipped with secure HF communications gear; the operator's workstation with the radios and the scrambler/descrambler was located in a special enclosure to starboard at the aft extremity of the cabin.

The other version has a combi layout with a forward cargo bay which can accommodate an inflatable dinghy. Aft of it are the crew toilet and the galley, followed by a cabin for the retinue with three rows of economy-class seats, a cabin for guests of honour with three rows of first class seats two-abreast, a wardrobe and a lavatory (to port and starboard respectively), the VIP cabin (identical to that of the first version) and the HF communications equipment operator's cubicle. Both versions have a crew of three (including a navigator).

Be-200P Patrol Amphibian (Project)

Although originally the Be-200 was designed and developed primarily for civil uses, it is quite capable of fulfilling useful tasks in military service – above all, as a patrol aircraft. The first such variant of the Be-200 amphibian, intended to perform various missions in the 200-mile EEZ, was studied by TANTK in 1996. The Be-200P patrol aircraft would be capable of fulfilling the following tasks:

• search for ships and vessels in a designated area, their classification and determination of their co-ordinates;
• visual reconnaissance of fishery gear;
• collecting documentary evidence of breaches of the established fishery rules;
• placing inspection groups on board trespasser vessels without summoning border guard ships (by alighting on water);
• the use (in case of need) of weapons against intruding vessels;
• ecological monitoring (including sea surface pollution monitoring), monitoring weather conditions and radiation levels;
• ice reconnaissance;
• participation in oil spill response actions;
• transportation of both personnel and cargoes;
• the paradropping of small groups of personnel.

The aircraft's flight and navigation avionics would enable it to follow automatically a predesignated route, as well as to determine the position, course and speed of surface tar-

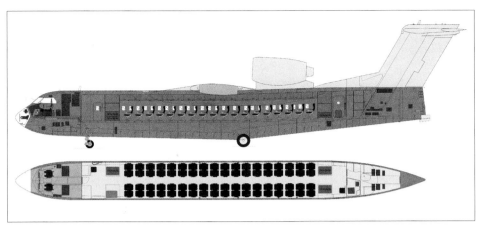

Above: The interior layout of the proposed Be-210 airliner amphibian.

An artist's impression of the Be-210; note the absence of the cargo door.

gets. The patrol version was be fitted with the Strizh (Martlet) radar enclosed by a longer, reshaped radome, reconnaissance equipment and additional communications equipment (which included an external acoustic address system with powerful loudspeakers, an automatic data link system for transmitting information to other aircraft and to ground-based or ship-based command posts). The aircraft featured six wing pylons enabling it to

carry podded reconnaissance equipment (for example, a thermal imager or a searchlight), as well as SAR capsules – or weapons.

In order to extend the Be-200P's range, its fuel load was increased by deleting part of the basic version's equipment (the water tanks and associated water scoop and vent system and so on). The crew complement could vary depending on the mission (up to nine, including the two pilots). In the event of long-

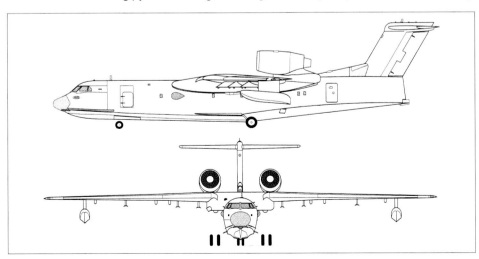

The Be-200P maritime patrol aircraft.

Above: In due course Be-200ChS RF-21515 was reregistered again, becoming RF-32515. Here it is shown on final approach; note the optronic 'ball turret'.

endurance patrol flights a relief crew could be carried in a rest compartment.

The Be-200P would be able to fulfil the whole range of its tasks in any season of the year, day and night, in simple and adverse weather at all geographic latitudes, including the Arctic regions; it would be based at airfields with a runway length of at least 1,800 m (5,900 ft), or at prepared airstrips near the coastline. Production of the Be-200P would, in effect, involve simply fitting the baseline version with the mission equipment and some insignificant changes in the structure of the hull and the wings; therefore, the patrol ver-

sion of the amphibian could be produced on the same assembly line as the standard Be-200/Be-200ChS.

Be-200PS SAR Amphibian (Project)

A further development of the Be-200P led to the emergence of the projected Be-200PS patrol/SAR aircraft. This version was to be provided with improved avionics for patrol and search duties, as well as SAR equipment (thermal imaging systems, a search radar, an observation/video recording system, a system for communication with coast guard units, rescue dinghies and rafts, and rescue

equipment). The crew of the Be-200PS would comprise two pilots, two observers, a flight engineer and two rescue workers.

Be-220 (Be-220P) Patrol Amphibian (Project)

This patrol aircraft based on the Be-200 amphibian appears to be an upgraded version of the Be-200P described above; presumably, this project features more advanced mission equipment and armament. According to reports in Western publications, the Be-220P (also referred to simply as Be-220) is to be armed with Kh-35U anti-shipping missiles and ASW torpedoes carried in an internal weapons bay or externally on six underwing pylons. The Be-220 will be fitted with the Novella mission equipment already tested on an upgraded version of the IL-38 ASW aircraft (in its export version, as fitted to the IL-38SD for the Indian Navy, this system is known as Sea Dragon).

The existence of this version has not yet been officially confirmed.

Be-250 AEW&C Aircraft (Project)

Practically nothing is known about this airborne early warning & control version, apart from a brief and vague mention in a Western publication. This airborne early warning and control aircraft was depicted in a side view drawing as fitted with a nose-mounted IFR probe and elongated bulged dielectric panels on the sides of the upper fuselage fore and aft of the wings. Again, this version has not yet made its appearance in TANTK advertising materials or Russian publications.

Be-200ChS RF-32516 displays its clean lines as it passes overhead. No 'ball turret' is fitted yet.

Chapter 5

On the Seven Seas

Ocean-Going Seaplane Projects

Supersonic Long-Range Maritime Bomber/Reconnaissance Aircraft

In keeping with Council of Ministers directive No.1119-582ss dated 15th August 1956 the Beriyev OKB undertook preliminary design work on a supersonic long-range maritime bomber/reconnaissance aircraft (no designation has been revealed). This was to be an amphibian intended both for joint operations with submarines and for independent operations on the ocean shipping lanes.

The aircraft was to be capable of taking off, alighting and staying afloat in the open sea in daytime and at night, under adverse weather conditions, in a sea state of 3 to 4 on the Beaufort scale. It was expected to rendezvous with 'friendly' submarines at designated points after a lengthy flight over water at long distances from the coast, to receive fuel from submarines and surface vessels in the open sea at a sea state of 3 to 4, to detect, identify and engage the target in daytime and at night under any weather conditions and in a strong ECM environment.

In accordance with the specification the seaplane was to be powered by 22,000-kgp (48,500-lbst) Kuznetsov NK-6 afterburning turbofans – the world's most powerful aero engine at the time. However, thorough analysis conducted in the course of the design work showed that the use of the more promising NK-10 engines would make it possible to create a machine with higher performance (see table); therefore, it was the NK-10 that was chosen for the final project version. With two fuel top-ups from a submarine, the range in supersonic cruise could be extended to 18,000-20,000 km (11,200-12,430 miles).

By the end of the 1950s several projects of advanced airborne combat systems that were under development in the Soviet Union were closed down due to Nikita Khrushchov's strong bias in favour of rocketry. Beriyev's supersonic long-range maritime bomber/ reconnaissance aircraft project also fell victim to the 'missile itch'.

The specifications of the aircraft are given in the tables on this page.

	CofM specifications with NK-6 engines	Design performance with NK-10 engines
Maximum speed at 10,000-11,000 m (32,810-36,090 ft), km/h (mph)	1,700-1,800 (1,057-1,119)	2,300-2,400 (1,429-1,492) *
Maximum range at subsonic speed (950 km/h; 590 mph), km (miles)	7,500-8,000 (4,661-4,972)	7,000-7,700 (4,350-4,786) †
Service ceiling above the target, m (ft)	15,000-16,000 (49,200-52,480)	20,000 (65,620)

* cruising speed; † at cruising speed

Design Performance of the Supersonic Long-Range Maritime Bomber/Reconnaissance Aircraft

Powerplant	4 x NK-10
Length	61.4 m (201 ft 5½ in)
Height	11.5 m (37 ft 8¾ in)
Wing span	26.4 m (86 ft 7½ in)
Wing area, m² (sq ft)	325 (3,499)
Maximum all-up weight, kg (lb)	240,000 (529,200)
Maximum fuel load, kg (lb)	186,000 (410,130)
Maximum useful load, kg (lb)	5,000 (11,025)
Cruising speed, km/h (mph)	2,440 (1,516)
Landing speed, km/h (mph)	290 (180)
Service ceiling, m (ft)	20,000 (65,600)
Range with maximum load, km (miles)	7,000-7,700 (4,350-4,786)
Crew	3

Above: An artist's impression of the supersonic reconnaissance/bomber flying boat. The fuselage-mounted engines have F-104 style half-cones in the air intakes. Note the dorsal weapons loading hatch.
Below: A cutaway drawing of the same aircraft, showing the anti-shipping cruise missile stowed internally and the retracted hydrofoils fore and aft of the weapons bay.

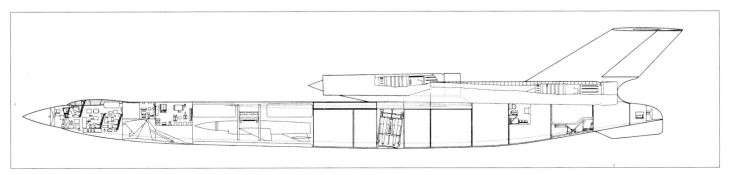

Above: An artist's impression of a large amphibian powered by four NK-8 turbofans. This project was, in effect, the forebear of the A-40; note the shoulder-mounted wings with tip-mounted outrigger floats.

Above and below: A different project featuring the same cruise engines but making use of mid-set gull wings of delta planform. The upper drawing shows the amphibian making use of lift engines buried in the thick wing roots. Oddly, the lower drawing shows no outrigger floats.

High-Speed Transport/ASW Amphibian with Four NK-8 Engines

This project (again, no designation is known) was under development in 1962. The amphibian was intended for delivering cargoes to combat ships and submarines at their deployment locations, as well as to Air Defence Force units stationed in remote areas of the Far East and High North. In addition, the aircraft could be modified into an SAR version with a 2,500-km (1,553-mile) radius of action

or into an ASW aircraft capable of performing its missions at a distance of 2,000-3,000 km (1,243-1,865 miles) from the base. It would be capable of being refuelled at sea and of performing its mission while staying afloat in the ASW patrol area.

The aircraft was designed as an amphibious flying boat with low-aspect-ratio delta wings and a swept-back T-tail. The mid-set gull wings were joined to the hull amidships. The aircraft was to have two pressurised cab-

Specifications of the Amphibious Aircraft Powered by Four NK-8 engines

Length, m (ft)	51.7 m (169 ft 7½ in)
Height, m (ft)	13.8 m (45 ft 3¼ in)
Wing span, m (ft)	40.0 m (131 ft 2¾ in)
Wing area, m² (sq ft)	430 (4,629)
Maximum take-off weight, kg (lb):	
from land	160,000 (352,800)
from water	145,000 (319,725)
Maximum payload, kg (lb)	40,000 (88,200)
Ordnance load, kg (lb)	6,000 (13,230)
Cruising speed, km/h (mph)	850 (528)
Landing speed, km/h (mph)	200 (124)
Service ceiling, m (ft)	14,000 (45,920)
Take-off run (land), m (ft)	1,800 (5,900)
Take-off run (water), m (ft)	2,000 (6,560)
Range with max. fuel, km (miles)	8,600 (5,345)
Range with max. payload, km (miles)	3,600 (2,237)
Endurance, hours	8
Crew	5-7

ins; the forward cabin accommodated five crew and 10-12 cargo attendants, the other one was a cargo cabin measuring 28 x 3.5 x 3 m (91 ft 10²³⁄₆₄ in x 11 ft 5¾ in x 9 ft 10 in). Loading and unloading was to be effected through a hatch in the aft part of the hull. The aircraft had a tricycle undercarriage; the four-wheel main gear bogies retracted aft into the wing centre section. The powerplant comprised four 9,500-kgp (20,940-lbst) Kuznetsov NK-8 non-afterburning turbofans placed in pairs on pylons above the wings.

LL-400 and LL-600 Ocean-Going Seaplanes

The projects of the LL-400 and LL-600 ocean-going seaplanes (LL = *letayushchaya lodka* – flying boat) having a take-off weight of some 400 tonnes (882,000 lb) and 600 tonnes (1,323,000 lb) respectively – hence the designations – were under development in the early 1960s. The LL-400 seaplane was projected from early 1963 onwards in several versions: a transport (the baseline version), an airliner and a long-range ASW/SAR aircraft. Subsequently the giant LL-600 served as a basis for a whole series of projected heavy flying boats intended for various roles.

The LL-400 and LL-600 seaplanes were heavy flying boats featuring a tailless delta layout. They had mid-set gull wings joined to the hull amidships and a swept-back vertical tail. The flightdeck and the cargo cabin (the latter measuring 60 x 8 x 5 m /197 ft x 26 ft 3 in x 16 ft 5 in on the LL-600) were pressurised. Loading and unloading took place through a hatch in the stern closed by clamshell doors and equipped with a vehicle loading ramp.

The powerplant of both seaplanes comprised eight NK-6 afterburning turbofans

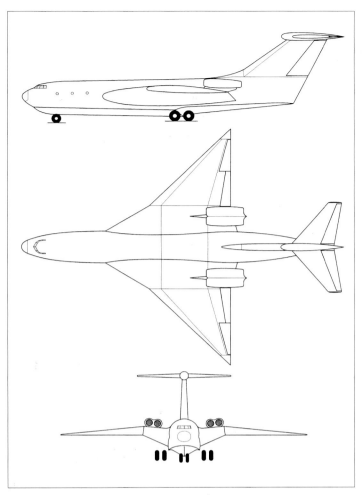
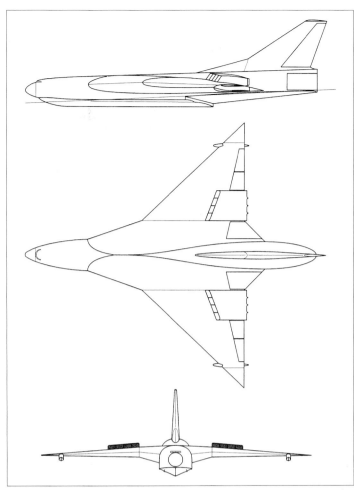

Above left: A three-view of the unnamed transport amphibian in its gull-wing version.
Above right: A three-view of the LL-600 flying boat.

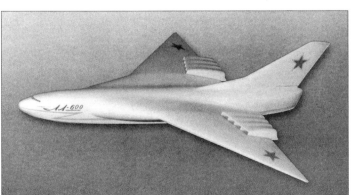

Left and above left: Artist's impressions of the LL-400 flying boat.
Above right, a model and, right, an artist's impression of the LL-600. The helicopter parked on top gives an idea of the size of this giant.

Specifications of the LL-600 Ocean-Going Seaplane

Length	82.6 m (271 ft 0 in)
Height	25 m (82 ft 0 in)
Wing span	76 m (249 ft 4¼ in)
Wing area, m² (sq ft)	744.5 (8,014.5)
Maximum all-up weight, tonnes (lb)	600 (1,323,000)
Maximum useful load, tonnes (lb)	300 (661,500)
Cruising speed, km/h (mph)	850 (528)
Landing speed, km/h (mph)	260 (162)
Service ceiling, m (ft)	17,000 (55,760)
Take-off run, m (ft)	3500 (11,480)
Range with a maximum fuel load, km (miles)	13,900 (8,639)
Range with a maximum useful load, km (miles)	2,000 (1,243)
Crew	12

located on the upper surface of the wings. On the LL-400 the engines were arranged in pairs, two pylon-mounted nacelles being located above the trailing edge of each wing and distributed spanwise. On the LL-600 the engines were grouped in packages of four, these packages being placed just outboard of the kink on the gull wings. The entire fuel load was carried in integral tanks in the wing torsion box.

A-150 Multi-Purpose Amphibian

The project of the A-150 multi-purpose ocean-going amphibious aircraft capable of operating from all kinds of airfields was developed in 1965. The seaplane was intended for detecting and destroying submarines in remote ocean areas, for laying mines and dropping Yauza sonobuoys (Yauza is the name of a river in the Moscow Region), for long-range photographic and electronic maritime reconnaissance, for SAR and assault/transport operations, and for destroying surface ships with air-to-surface missiles. In addition to these roles, there were plans to develop an IFR tanker version. Furthermore, the amphibian could be used in the national economy for the transportation of urgent cargoes and for supporting the fishing fleet. The A-150 was to operate from dirt airstrips with a bearing strength of 4-6 kg/cm² (57-85 lb/sq in), with a runway length of 600-800 m (1,970-2,620 ft), as well as from water at a sea state of 4 to 5. Ice airstrips could be used when operating in the Arctic region. The powerplant comprised four NK-8 turbofans as the cruise engines, augmented by twelve Kolesov RD36-35P lift turbojets to assist take-off.

The structural layout of the A-150 reflected the amphibian's multi-role concept. It could be used in the following versions: an

ASW aircraft with a system of sonobuoys; an ASW aircraft with a dunking sonar; an aircraft for setting up minefields and sonobuoy barriers; an IFR tanker; a maritime reconnaissance/target designator aircraft; an SAR aircraft; a troop and cargo carrier, and a missile strike aircraft. To minimise the time required for preparing the aircraft for this or that mission, provision was made for interchangeable mission equipment pods with a total volume of 30 m³ (1,060 cu ft); they were suspended in two bays in the wing centre section. The pods had standardised attachment fittings. The wing cargo bays were to be outfitted with appropriate couplings and connectors for the electrical wiring, hydraulic and pneumatic piping. Part of the equipment was placed in the crew cabin; it was replaced concurrently with the replacement of the pods.

The A-150DT troop carrier/transport amphibian (*desahntno-tranhsportnyy* – assault/transport, used attributively) differed from the baseline version in having an entirely new boat hull of bigger dimensions (49.2 m/161 ft 5 in long and 4.8 m/15 ft 9 in wide) featuring a large 'tailgate'; the wing centre section contours were partially changed. The number of RD36-35P lift engines was increased from 12 to 16 (a conventional take-off/vertical landing version equipped with 32

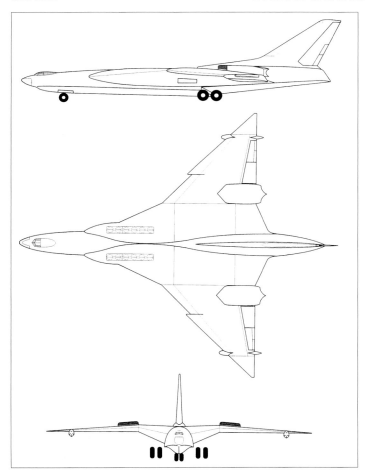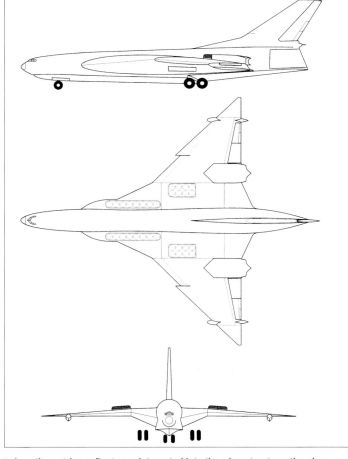

Three-views of the A-150 multi-role amphibian (left) and the A-150DT transport. Note how the outrigger floats are integrated into the wing structure; the plan views show the location of the lift engines.

Specifications of the A-150 Amphibian

Powerplant (cruise engines)	4 x NK-8
Engine thrust, kg (lb)	4 x 9,500
	(4 x 20,950)
Powerplant (lift engines)	12 x RD-36-35P
Engine thrust, kg (lb)	12 x 3,700
	(12 x 8,160)
Length	49.8 m (163 ft 4⅝ in)
Height on ground	12.8 m (42 ft 0 in)
Wing span	42.0 m (137 ft 9³⁵⁄₆₄ in)
Wing area, m² (sq ft)	500 (5,382)
Maximum TOW (water), kg (lb)	150,000 (330,750)
Maximum TOW (land), kg (lb)	170,000 (374,850)
Maximum fuel load (water), kg (lb)	80,000 (176,400)
Maximum fuel load (land), kg (lb)	100,000 (220,500)
Maximum useful load, kg (lb)	5,000 (11,025)
Cruising speed, km/h (mph)	900 (559)
Landing speed, km/h (mph)	137 (85)
Service ceiling, m (ft)	15,000 (49,200)
Range with max fuel, km (miles)	11,750 (7,302)
Endurance, hours	10.3
Crew	5

Above: An artist's impression of the A-150 in its baseline form. Note the open intake scoops of the lift-jets; each intake serves two engines.

lift-jets was also envisaged). In this case the airframe weight was increased by 6,600 kg (14,550 lb). The cargo compartment measured 32 x 3.5 x 3.4 m (105 ft x 11 ft 6 in x 11 ft 2 in); the maximum cargo lifting capacity was 30,000 kg (66,150 lb). The armament comprised two powered turrets with AO-19 cannons (nose- and stern-mounted), with a total complement of 2,000 rounds for both turrets, including PIKS infrared decoy rounds and PRLS rounds filled with chaff.

Be-800, Be-1000, Be-2000, Be-2000P, Be-2500, Be-2500P and Be-5000 Heavy Ocean-Going Seaplanes/WIG Aircraft

In parallel with the work on current tasks, the Beriyev OKB in co-operation with TsAGI, the Central Aero Engine Institute (TsIAM – *Tsentrahl'nyy institoot aviatsionnovo motorostroyeniya*) and the Siberian Aviation Research Institute named after S. A. Chaplygin (SibNIA – *Sibeerskiy naoochno-issledovatel'skiy institoot aviahtsii*) in Novosibirsk has pursued scientific research and design work on ultra-heavy seaplanes intended for various missions. The need for research in this direction is determined by the fact that, besides having higher performance, large seaplanes also have better seaworthiness. Studies have been made of the possible areas where seaplanes with an all-up weight in excess of 300 tonnes (660,000 lb) can be operated; they have shown that it will be possible to operate such machines at sea states with waves more than 5 m (16 ft) high all year round in the world ocean areas in southern latitudes with a probability of up to 80-95%, and in northern areas of the Atlantic and the Pacific with a probabil-

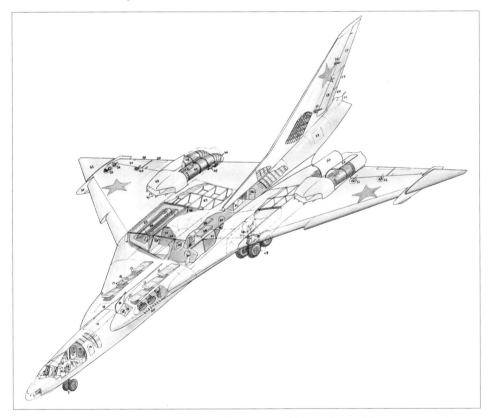

This cutaway drawing of the A-150 shows the ordnance bays which may be used for weapons or mission equipment pods. Note the movable deflectors directing the exhaust jets downwards to assist take-off.

ity of up to 60-70% in winter and 90-95% in summer. The main missions performed by ultra-heavy seaplanes may comprise transoceanic transportation of cargoes and passengers, transport operations in the high seas, and SAR missions. Operation of ultra-heavy amphibians will call for minimal alterations in the infrastructure of the ports under construction or modernisation, requiring only the enlargement of dams protecting the sea-

Above: The D2 flying model designed to explore the aerodynamic and hydrodynamic properties of the layout chosen for the family of ultra-heavy seaplanes.

Above: A display model of the Be-2500 Class C WIG craft capable of high-altitude flight. The exhaust of the four engines mounted on the foreplanes is directed under the wings to create an air cushion.

An artist's impression of a Be-2500 moored at a special loading dock. Note how the cargo bays in the wing trailing-edge sections are loaded across the entire width; the main cabin is accessed via the tailcone.

ports' water areas intended for seaplane operations, and the construction of seaplane slipways and parking areas. When compared to the huge expenses planned for the construction of new airports, the funds required for such adaptation of the port infrastructure will be insignificant.

The concept of ultra-heavy amphibious aircraft, as evolved by designers of the Beriyev TANTK, comprises the following basic ideas:

• the aircraft must be capable of performing a take-off at a minimum all-up weight from a land airfield or come out of the water onto the slipway under its own power;

• providing space for landing gear stowage on ultra-heavy aircraft with an all-up weight in excess of 500 tonnes (1,102,500 lb) presents considerable difficulties and entails a reduction of the payload/weight ratio; on amphibians featuring high-set wings the weight penalty incurred by the tall undercarriage may be even greater. For this reason the adopted concept envisages a low-wing amphibian with an undercarriage stressed for a minimum weight that is required for ensuring flights over the distances of 500-700 km (310-435 miles) or for enabling the empty aircraft to come out onto the slipway.

The main technical features of this concept were studied in the course of projecting the 'D' (A-70) and P-2 amphibians, which were to make use of the ground effect in the take-off and landing modes. On the basis of the results thus obtained, the Beriyev TANTK developed a series of projected ultra-heavy Class C wing-in-ground effect (WIG) craft making use of the ground effect for enhancing their take-off and landing properties but performing cruise flight in the usual aeroplane mode. These projects comprised machines with different all-up weights reflected in their designations: the Be-800 (800 tonnes; 1,763,670 lb), Be-1000 (1,000 tonnes; 2,204585 lb), Be-2000 (2,000 tonnes; 4,409,170 lb), Be-2500 (2,500 tonnes; 5,511,460 lb) and Be-5000 (5,000 tonnes; 11,025,000 lb). The engines considered as powerplants for these craft included the indigenous Kuznetsov NK-62M and NK-116 prospective turbofans and the British Rolls-Royce Trent turbofan.

The Be-1000 amphibian features a flying-wing layout with twin vertical tails. The wingtips are canted upwards; they are movable, acting as flight control surfaces. Seven NK-62M cruise engines mounted above the wing centre section endow the amphibian with a maximum cruising speed of up to 600 km/h (373 mph). The undercarriage comprises a nose unit, the main units and supporting units with six-wheel-bogies.

The three-spar wings having an area of 1,930 m² (20,776 sq ft) blend integrally into the hull to form a single lifting body featuring transverse and longitudinal steps; the leading-edge sweepback is 50°. The water displacing volumes are contained both in the hull and in the wings (that is, the wings rest on the water and act as stabilising floats when the craft is afloat), as is the case with the Be-103 six-seat light amphibian.

The forward part of the hull houses the flightdeck for five crew; placed beneath it is an equipment bay and the nosewheel well. The passengers are accommodated in the pressurised part of the hull extending to the front wing spar; six passenger cabins are placed on two decks and are provided with emergency exits, galleys and toilets.

The unpressurised sections of the airframe (in the wings and the double-deck hull) house cargo compartments which are provided with a cargo floor, cargo handling devices and tiedown cleats. The cargo compartments have clamshell doors measuring 2.6 x 3.1 m (8 ft 6 in x 10 ft 2 in) and located behind the rear wing spar. The fuel is housed in the wings (in the leading-edge sections and above the cargo compartments. The Be-1000 can transport a maximum useful load of up to 600 tonnes (1,323,000 lb).

The 2,000-ton Be-2000 passenger/cargo seaplane was projected in two versions, one of which featured devices deflecting the engine exhaust under the wings to create an air cushion (the other version was more conventional). There were also several variants differing in the engine arrangement and wing layout.

In the layout making use of the jet-augmented air cushion (called Be-2000P, the suffix denoting *poddoov* = wing blowing), six NK-62M engines are mounted on swivelling horizontal pylons flanking the forward part of the hull. A further four engines are mounted on the aft portion of the wing centre section or on pylons attached to the vertical tails. The swivelling forward pylons act as canard foreplanes. In cruise flight the engines mounted on the foreplanes function as normal propulsion engines. In the layout lacking the exhaust blowing feature (the Be-2000 *sans suffixe*) twelve NK-62M engines are mounted on pylons above the upper wing surface.

In one of the layouts the Be-2000's wings have a centre section of large dimensions incorporating cargo compartments with a total volume of 2,700 m³ (95,363 cu ft). Such wings can house a considerable part of the payload and fuel. Loading/unloading is done through full-width cargo hatches in the trailing-edge section of the wings. In another layout the wings feature a high aspect ratio, variable thickness along the span and a centre section of a small volume holding only fuel.

The aircraft's hull has a double-deck layout. The upper deck accommodates the flightdeck, passenger cabins seating 730 passengers, and auxiliary compartments (the kitchen, galleys, wardrobes and toilets). The lower deck serves as a cargo cabin measuring 88 x 8 x 4 m (288 ft 9 in x 26 ft 3 in x 13 ft 1½ in). In the SAR version both passenger and cargo cabins can be converted for the transportation of persons recovered during rescue operations.

Cargoes can be loaded and unloaded via three hatches. The front hatch is formed by raising the hinged nose visor of the boat hull and deploying a cargo ramp (in the manner of the Antonov An-124 Ruslan or the Lockheed C-5 Galaxy). The rear one is closed by clamshell doors forming the aft end of the hull; the third hatch is located dorsally in the aft hull decking, allowing loading and unloading by crane even when no compatible quay is available. Passengers board and disembark via entry doors in the hull's sides.

In the SAR version, rescuees can be lifted aboard through special hatches in the wing leading edge. The double-deck cabin provides accommodation for 544 heavily wounded persons and up to 1,214 rescuees.

The aircraft has a crew of five: two pilots, a navigator, a flight engineer and a loadmaster. In the SAR version a team of rescue workers and medical personnel is also carried.

The Be-2500, a giant six-engined seaplane using the ground effect and having a take-off weight of 2,500 tonnes, is intended for commercial transportation of passengers and cargoes on intercontinental routes. It has been repeatedly demonstrated in model form at various international airshows. As conceived by the designers, the seaplane can perform flights both at high altitudes (8,000-12,000 m; 26,250-39,370 ft) and in WIG mode near the water surface at a height of 4-10 m (13-33 ft). The Be-2500 features a flying-wing layout with twin T-tails incorporating the concept of water-displacing wings, which permits aquaplaning with the machine resting on three points. Four of the engines are mounted on canard foreplanes and the other two on top of the wings. Take-off from water is to be performed making use of an augmented air cushion: the efflux of the engines mounted on the forward fuselage is directed under the wings where, trapped in a confined space, it forms an air cushion helping to lift the aircraft off the water.

Propulsion is to be provided either by the prospective Kuznetsov NK-116 turbofans with a fan diameter of 5 m (16 ft 5 in) developed by the Samara-based SNTK Trood ('Labour' Science & Production Enterprise), or by Rolls-Royce Trent engines delivering a thrust of 45,000 kgp (99,275 lbst) apiece. The Be-2500 is provided with a retractable beaching gear which is not suitable for flights from land.

Again, the fuselage has a double-deck layout. The upper deck accommodates the flightdeck, passenger cabins seating 73 passengers, and auxiliary compartments. The lower deck houses a cargo cabin measuring 96 x 9 x 4.6 m (315 ft x 29 ft 6 in x 15 ft). It can also be converted for passenger transportation; in this case the overall seating capacity can reach 1,600.

Of course, such a mammoth aircraft as the Be-2500 can only materialise in the distant future – all the more so since construction of such machines cannot be tackled by any single country alone and calls for joint efforts within the framework of various international projects. However, the research and development potential accumulated in Russia, multiplied by the modern state-of-the-art in aero engine construction, aircraft materials and avionics, gives reasons to hope that aircraft of that kind will be able to bring about a combination of air and marine transportation within a joint transport system and will eventually prove to be more efficient in comparison with marine transport, harmoniously adapting themselves to the already existing infrastructure of seaports.

Specifications of the Be-2500 Seaplane

Wing area, m² (sq ft)	3,428 (36,902)
Maximum all-up weight, tonnes (lb)	2,500 (5,512,500)
Maximum useful load, tonnes (lb)	1,000 (2,205,000)
Powerplant	12 x Rolls-Royce Trent
Engine thrust, kg (lb)	12 x 45,000 (12 x 99,275)
Cruising speed in high-altitude flight (H=10 km/32,810 ft), km/h (mph)	800 (497)
Cruising speed in WIG mode, km/h (mph)	450 (280)
Take-off speed, km/h (mph)	420 (261)
Take-off run, m (ft)	15,000 (49,200)
Ferrying range in WIG mode, km (miles)	10,700 (6,650)
Ferrying range in high-altitude flight, km (miles)	17,000 (10,565)
Seaworthiness (wind-induced wave height), m (ft)	5 (16.4)
Seating capacity	up to 1,600

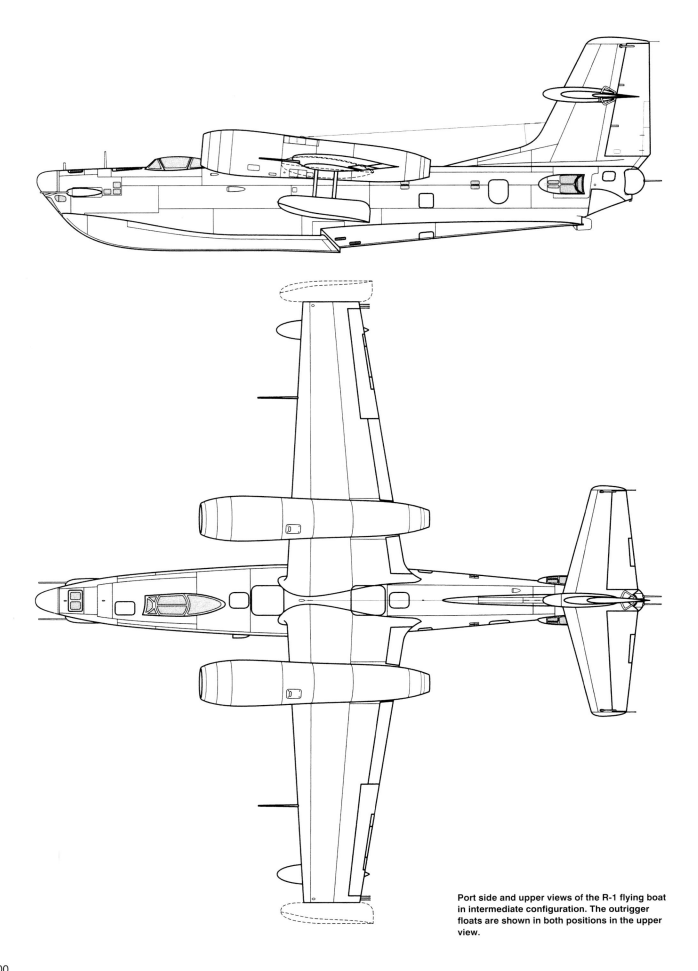

Port side and upper views of the R-1 flying boat in intermediate configuration. The outrigger floats are shown in both positions in the upper view.

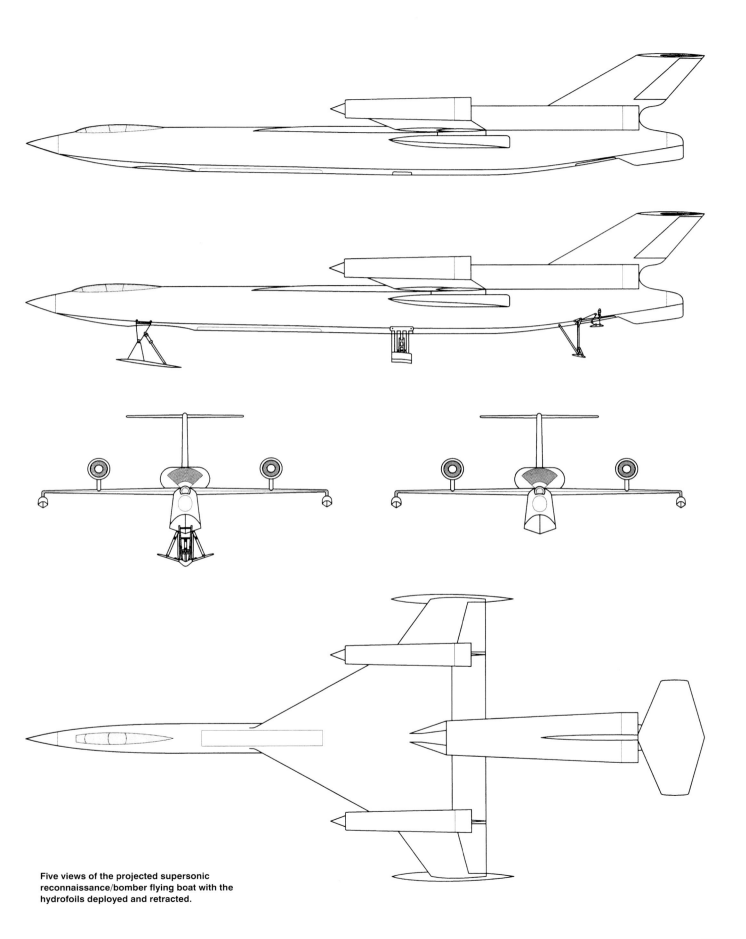

Five views of the projected supersonic reconnaissance/bomber flying boat with the hydrofoils deployed and retracted.

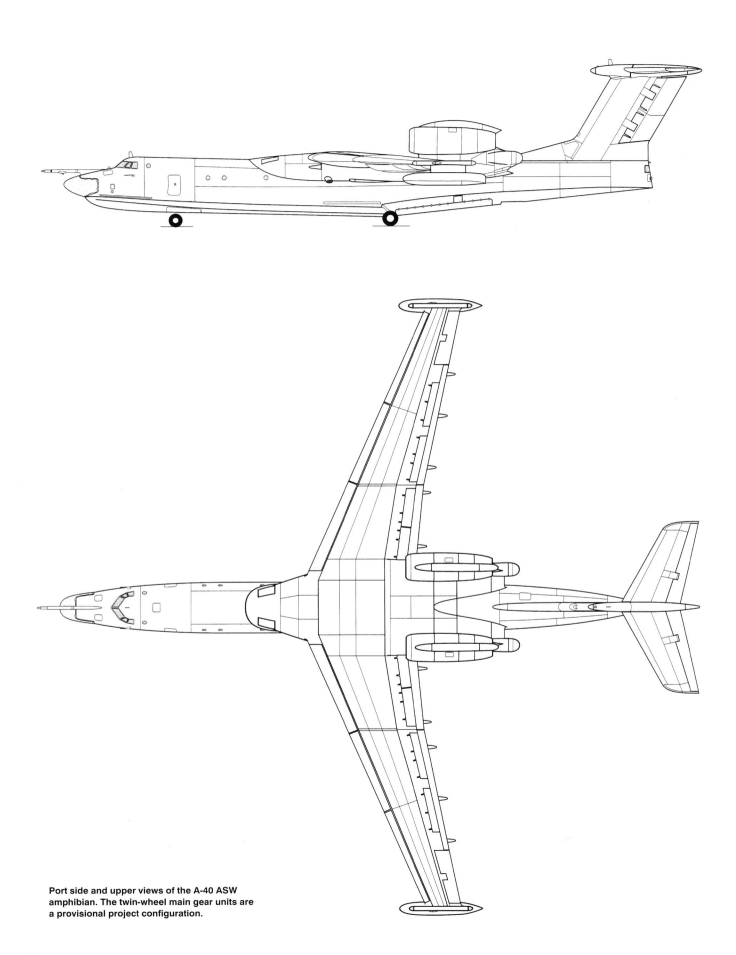

Port side and upper views of the A-40 ASW
amphibian. The twin-wheel main gear units are
a provisional project configuration.

106

Above: The Beriyev OKB started exploring wing-in-ground effect (WIG) vehicles operated from water in the early 1960s. The first result of this research was the GL-1 (alias Be-1) turbojet-powered subscale demonstrator of 1965. (This vehicle was described in Red Star Vol.8: *Russia's Ekranoplans*.)

'10 Red', the prototype of the Be-10 flying boat.

Above: The first production Be-10, '15 Red' (c/n 8600101). Note the photo calibration markings.

Another aspect of the first production Be-10 anchored at Ghelendjik Bay.

Above: '40 Yellow' (c/n 0600505), the Be-10 used for setting 12 world speed, altitude and payload records in September 1961. The tail fairing is clearly visible.

Another view of the record-breaking Be-10 (M-10) preparing to take off.

Above: '10 Red' (*izdeliye* V1), the first prototype of the A-40 Albatross ASW amphibian, in its ultimate colour scheme.

The first prototype A-40 commences its take-off run. Note the deployed slats and aft trim.

Above: Another view of '10 Red' immediately before becoming airborne.

The second prototype ('20 Red', *izdeliye* V2) in its current colour scheme is pushed back by an APA-100 ground power unit on a Ural-4320 chassis.

Above: '20 Red' leaves the slipway at Ghelendjik and taxies out during the Hydro Aviation Show-98 in September 1998.

The second prototype A-40 takes off on a demonstration flight at the Ghelendjik show.

Above: The A-40's hull and the efflux of its D-30KPV cruise engines and RD-36-35 boosters create huge plumes of spray during take-off.

The second prototype alights after a demonstration flight.

Above: The second prototype A-40 in the static display at the Hydro Aviation Show-98.

Still wearing the original cheatline and the Le Bourget exhibit code 378, the second prototype makes a demonstration flight at the MAKS-93 airshow.

Above: The first prototype Be-200 takes off on its maiden flight on 24th September 1998, showing the deployed ram air turbine on the fin fillet.

The first prototype was unpainted and unregistered during the first three flights.

Above: The first prototype (RA-21511) makes the Be-200's first take-off from water at Taganrog on 10th September 1999.

The Be-200 banks away after delivering a firebombing demonstration; a pall of water droplets streams from the open discharge doors in the planing bottom.

Above: Now wearing the exhibit code 377, RA-21511 demonstrates its ability to take on and offload cargoes when afloat. Note the EMERCOM of Russia badge ahead of the cargo door.

The Be-200's most spectacular show piece – a firebombing demonstration with the water dyed in Russian flag colours.

Above: RA-21512, the Be-200ChS prototype, afloat at Ghelendjik on 3rd September 2002. The grey colour scheme is livened up a bit by Beriyev, BETAIR JSC, IAPO and EMERCOM of Russia logos on the fuselage.

The landing gear struts churn up the waves as the Be-200ChS prepares to come ashore. RA-21512 was an unexpected and thus all the more welcome visitor to the Hydro Aviation Show-2002.

Above: RA-21512 shows off its bright blue hull bottom and outrigger float bottoms. The Be-200 is an elegant aircraft when airborne.

Another view of the Be-200ChS prototype on a demonstration flight.

Above: Displaying its original registration RA-21515, the first production Be-200ChS takes off from runway 12 at Zhukovskiy. The machine looks great in EMERCOM colours.

Here, the landing gear is caught in mid-retraction; the nose unit retracts faster.

Above: Now displaying its current identity (RF-32515), the same aircraft is seen on short finals.

RA-21515 scoops up water as it skims along the surface of the Moskva River just outside the airfield boundary at Zhukovskiy.

We hope you enjoyed this book . . .

Midland Publishing titles are edited and designed by an experienced and enthusiastic team of specialists.

We always welcome ideas from authors or readers for books they would like to see published.

In addition, our associate, Midland Counties Publications, offers an exceptionally wide range of aviation, military, naval and transport books and videos for sale by mail-order worldwide.

For a copy of the appropriate catalogue, or to order further copies of this book, and any other Midland Publishing titles, please write, telephone, fax or e-mail to:

Midland Counties Publications
4 Watling Drive, Hinckley,
Leics, LE10 3EY, England
Tel: (+44) 01455 254 450
Fax: (+44) 01455 233 737
E-mail: midlandbooks@compuserve.com
www.midlandcountiessuperstore.com

US distribution by Specialty Press – see page 2.

Earlier titles in the series:

Vols 1, 3 to 11 are still available
Vol.12: Antonov's Turboprop Twins
Vol.13: Mikoyan's Piston-Engined Fighters
Vol.14: Mil Mi-8/Mi-17
Vol.15: Antonov An-2
Vol.16: Sukhoi Interceptors
Vol.17: Early Soviet Jet Bombers
Vol.18: Antonov's Heavy Transports
Vol.19: Soviet Heavy Interceptors
Vol.20: Soviet/Russian UAVs

Red Star Volume 21
ANTONOV'S JET TWINS
The An-72/-74 Family

Yefim Gordon and Dmitriy Komissarov

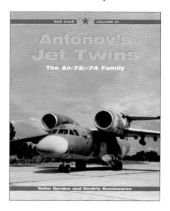

The need to provide a state-of-the-art jet successor to the An-26 led Antonov to develop a twin-turbofan tactical airlifter, the An-72, with its signature high-mounted engines employing the Coanda effect to dramatically improve wing lift and STOL capability.

The prototype flew in 1977 but it was not until the mid-1980s that production began. Comprehensive listings, both of An-72s and An-74s, detail registration/Bort number, c/n, f/n and operator.

Softback, 280 x 215 mm, 128 pages
125 colour, 90 b/w photographs,
4pp of line drawings
1 85780 199 7 **£19.99**

Red Star Volume 22
MIL'S HEAVYLIFT HELICOPTERS

Y Gordon, S & D Komissarov

The prototype Mil' Mi-6 heavy transport and assault helicopter first flew in 1957. In 1959 it served as the basis for the unconventional Mi-10. In 1967, Mil' amazed the world with the mighty V-12 capable of lifting a 25-ton payload; then in 1977 the OKB achieved success with the smaller but more advanced Mi-26, the world's largest production helicopter. The development history, design and civil and military use of all three types is described in detail.

Softback, 280 x 215 mm, 128 pages
174 b/w photographs, 21pp of colour,
10pp of line drawings
1 85780 206 3 **£19.99**

Red Star Volume 23
SOVIET/RUSSIAN AWACS AIRCRAFT

Yefim Gordon and Dmitriy Komissarov

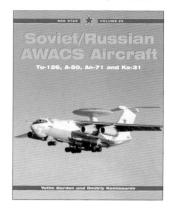

The need for effective protection of Soviet airspace in areas lacking adequate cover by ground radars led to work on airborne early warning systems. The Tu-126 AEW aircraft, evolved from the Tu-114 airliner, entered service in 1961. It was replaced in the early 1980s by the Ilyushin/Beriev A-50 AWACS based on the IL-76MD. The highly unorthodox An-71 with its tail-mounted rotodome and the Ka-31 AEW helicopter are also described plus other unbuilt projects.

Softback, 280 x 215 mm, 128 pages
144 colour, 70 b/w photographs,
plus 5pp of line drawings
1 85780 215 2 **£19.99**

Red Star Volume 24
TUPOLEV Tu-144
Russia's Concorde

Yefim Gordon and Vladimir Rigmant

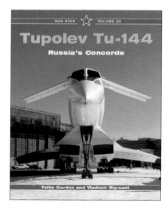

Tasked with creating a supersonic transport ahead of the West as a matter of national prestige, Andrey Tupolev met the target at the cost of a tremendous research and development effort. The Tu-144 took to the air in December 1968, ahead of the Anglo-French Concorde. This detailed account includes the reasons behind its premature withdrawal and a description of its recent use in a joint research programme with NASA.

Softback, 280 x 215 mm, 128 pages
151 b/w photos, 15 pages of colour
plus drawings
1 85780 216 0 **£19.99**

Red Star Volume 25
ILYUSHIN IL-12 & IL-14
Successors to the Li-2

Yefim Gordon and Dmitry Komissarov

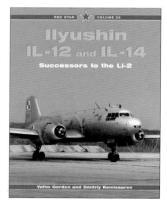

Designed to supersede the Li-2, the 29-seat IL-12 airliner entered Aeroflot service in 1948. Some 600 were built for Aeroflot and the Soviet armed forces. The improved IL-14 entered production in 1953, the type was exported to China, Bulgaria, Romania and Poland as well as being built by VEB in East Germany and Asia in Czechoslovakia. The total production of over 1,000 aircraft included 203 Avia 14s and Avia 14 Supers – the latter being a pressurised development.

Softback, 280 x 215 mm, 128 pages
180 b/w photos, 16 pages of colour
plus 12 pages of drawings
1 85780 223 3 **£19.99**

Red Star Volume 26
RUSSIA'S MILITARY AIRCRAFT IN THE 21st CENTURY

Yefim Gordon

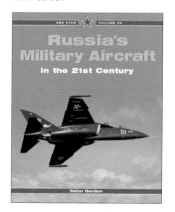

While the large new aircraft programmes of the Cold War era are a thing of the past, military aviation in Russia is not standing still. This volume looks at programmes like the new Mi-8MTKO and Mi-24PN night-capable helicopters, the latest Sukhoi upgrades such as the Su-24M2, Su-25SM and Su-27SM, new and more capable missiles for the Tu-95MS and Tu-160 bombers and the revamping of the training fleet with the Yak-130.

Softback, 280 x 215 mm, 128 pages
269 full colour photographs,
plus line drawings
1 85780 224 1 **£19.99**

Red Star Volume 27
LISUNOV Li-2
The Soviet DC-3

Yefim Gordon and Dmitry Komissarov

When they bought a manufacturing licence for the DC-3 in 1936, Soviet decision makers had no way of knowing the place the Douglas airliner would come to occupy in aviation's hall of fame. Adapted to employ Russian engines and materials, the DC-3 entered production as the PS-84; later redesignated Li-2. This addition to the series explores what is probably the least-known aspect of the history of one of the world's best-known airliners.

Softback, 280 x 215 mm, 128 pages
235 b/w photographs, plus
12 pages of colour
1 85780 228 4 **£19.99**